WINNING MANUFACTURING

WINNING MANUFACTURING

THE HOW-TO BOOK OF
SUCCESSFUL MANUFACTURING

JAMES A. TOMPKINS, PH.D.
TOMPKINS ASSOCIATES, INC.

INDUSTRIAL ENGINEERING & MANAGEMENT PRESS
NORCROSS, GEORGIA

The Library of Congress has catalogued this work as follows:

Tompkins, James A.
    Winning manufacturing : the how-to book of successful
manufacturing / James A. Tompkins.
        p.___ cm.___
    Includes bibliographical references.
    ISBN 0-89806-103-2 (pbk.):
    1. Production management. I. Title.
TS155.T57   1989   89-19811
                                                             CIP

96 95 94 93   7 6 5 4

Additional copies may be obtained by contacting:
Institute of Industrial Engineers
Customer Service
25 Technology Park/Atlanta
Norcross, Georgia 30092 USA
(404) 449-0460 phone
(404) 263-8532 fax

Quantity discounts available.

To my mother and my father, who passed away while this book was being written. Without a doubt, my understanding of winning came from Evelyn A. Tompkins and Carroll A. Tompkins. This book is dedicated to their winning memory.

TABLE OF CONTENTS

LIST OF FIGURES

LIST OF TABLES

FOREWORD

There is nothing new in this book. As pages are turned and facts, principles, and guidelines are presented, you will have a tendency to nod as if to say "Yes, this is true." So why read *Winning Manufacturing?* Because this book presents a sound approach to achieving manufacturing success. This book will make a real difference in your manufacturing operation.

There are no fads here, no three-letter words. What you find here is a focus on the things that need to be done for a manufacturing enterprise to succeed. In a sense, *Winning Manufacturing* is "back to basics" on a broad scale. The basics here, however, are not the basic functions of the manufacturing organization, but the basic requirements of manufacturing success, together with a "how-to" approach that will lead a manufacturing team to success.

This book is really about the integration of functions to create efficient and effective manufacturing systems. It considers the totality of manufacturing and identifies the critical requirements that must be done well.

There are no new fads here because none are needed. There are no quick fixes or panaceas in manufacturing. Fads, quick fixes, and panaceas don't work. Successful manufacturing comes from people who understand manufacturing and design manufacturing systems that are able to meet the manufacturing requirements presented in this book.

If an outcome is not a consequence of design, then it happened by accident. The design of the total manufacturing system has received too little attention. As much as we make of CIM, CAD/CAM/CAE, JIT, TQC, and so forth, these are band-aids if they are not applied within the design of the total system. This book presents an approach for achieving successful manufacturing. Companies that implement winning manufacturing will, in fact, win.

Del Kimbler, Ph.D., P.E.
President, Society of Integrated Manufacturing
Professor, Clemson University

PREFACE

In March 1987 I presented a talk, "The Challenge of Integrated Manufacturing" six times during a three-week period. The main points of this talk included:

1. The United States is the leader in the world manufacturing productivity race.
2. The wealth of a nation is directly related to its manufacturing success.
3. The acronym-chasing, management by fad approach that had been adopted by many companies has resulted in chaos. Manufacturing companies must adopt a consistent manufacturing strategy.

During these three weeks, I was asked the same question four times: "What consistent manufacturing strategy should be adopted?" Each time I answered, I gave a more in-depth response. After mulling over these responses, I decided I needed to spend some time specifically reflecting on the future direction of manufacturing.

I spent several days evaluating the essential elements of successful manufacturing, and several more days reviewing problems, opportunities, challenges, and failures of manufacturing. The result was a list of 156 requirements for success in manufacturing. I shared this list with the management team of Tompkins Associates, Inc., and we increased the list to 173 requirements. Through a simplification process, I reduced the list to 140, 96, 53, 41 and finally to 25 requirements that defined where manufacturing was headed.

With the help of a friend, Bernie Knill, the editor of *Material Handling Engineering*, I wrote a four-part series on the requirements of success in manufacturing. I also made many presentations on these requirements. The public's tremendous response indicated that manufacturing management desperately needed more information on these requirements. I realized I needed to disseminate this information. One step was the development of a video tape on success in manufacturing.

Dale Harmelink of Tompkins Associates, Inc. produced a video tape. We were overwhelmed by the requests for the video. The actual demand was five times higher than our projections. In July 1988, it became clear that I needed to write this book.

Winning Manufacturing is a composite of several hundred successful consulting projects, and of several hundred hours of putting onto paper the answers to the following questions:

1. Where should manufacturing be headed?
2. How should you improve your manufacturing operation?

As the title indicates, *Winning Manufacturing* is a how-to book written for the manufacturing manager and addresses all phases of manufacturing from product development to inventories, to marketing.

The material presented in this book works. I recommend that you read this book and implement winning manufacturing.

ACKNOWLEDGEMENTS

Special recognition should go to the people mentioned here for their support of this book.

Kim Perdue for her rough typing and Ashley Bowyer for her final typing, proofreading, and management of the manuscript; Carey Gifford and Maura Reeves of the Institute of Industrial Engineers' editorial staff for their dedicated support of this book; Mike Cramer, Larry Gould, Glen Mehltretter, and Jerry Smith who reviewed and edited early drafts of this book; Frank Daly, Dale Harmelink, Mike Miller, Dave Olson, and Eric Peters, the Tompkins Associates, Inc. management team, for the experiences we have shared; my partners at Tompkins Associates, Inc.; Rick Barnhill for his understanding of implementation, Jerry Smith for his clear thinking, and John Spain for his customer orientation, and the entire staff of Tompkins Associates, Inc. for their loyalty, trust, and confidence; and my children for their love–Tiffany for putting up with me, Jamie for being so happy, and Jimmy for asking "After you finish a chapter, Dad, can we play ball?"

Most of all, I would like to thank my wife. Shari Tompkins should be the subject of a book titled *Winning Wives*. Shari has been and will continue to be my confidant, sounding-board, editor, friend, and lover. Without Shari, there would be no *Winning Manufacturing*.

James A. Tompkins, Ph.D.
Raleigh, North Carolina
September 15, 1989

Chapter 1
WINNING MANUFACTURING

SUCCESSFUL MANUFACTURING OPERATIONS MUST BE BASED UPON A LONG-TERM COMMITMENT TO A BROAD-BASED, COMMON SENSE, STRUCTURED PROCESS OF CONTINUOUS IMPROVEMENT.

Winning manufacturing is a never-ending journey toward continuous improvement. A company that adopts the process of winning manufacturing will:

1. Produce quality products,
2. Have satisfied customers,
3. Identify manufacturing as a strategic strength,
4. Be profitable and growing, and
5. Be respected.

Winning manufacturing must be based upon a consistent direction, shared by the entire organization, of where manufacturing is headed. Achieving an organization-wide understanding of where a company is headed takes time. In a large manufacturing organization, it may take as long as two years to reach those on the shop floor. When management changes its view of where manufacturing operations should head, there is a ripple effect throughout the organization; some areas are working on management's manufacturing direction of a year ago, some of three months ago, and so on.

To assess how well your management has presented a consistent manufacturing direction, consider the variety of programs presented in Table 1 that have been pursued in the 1980s. Although the programs are valid and useful, the managerial shifting from one program to another has confused the work force. To achieve manufacturing success, these programs must be replaced by the singular process of winning manufacturing.

TABLE 1
Manufacturing Programs Of The 1980s

TOPIC	MANUFACTURING PROGRAM
Participative Management	Employee Involvement Job Enlargement Job Enrichment Organizational Development Quality Circles Quality of Work Life Team Building T Groups Theory X, Y and Z Total Preventative Maintenance
Product Development	Concurrent Engineering Design for Assembly Design for Manufacture Failure Mode and Effect Analysis Group Technology Mechatronics Simultaneous Engineering Taguchi Methods Value Analysis
Computerization	Artificial Intelligence Computer-Aided Design Computer-Aided Engineering Computer-Aided Inspection Computer-Aided Manufacturing Computer Integrated Manufacturing Manufacturing Resource Planning Material Requirements Planning
Manufacturing Themes	Continuous Flow Manufacturing Factory of the Future Factory with a Future Flexible Manufacturing Systems Focused Factories Just-In-Time Kanban Plant Within a Plant Synchronous Manufacturing Total Quality Control Zero Inventory

THIS BOOK IS ABOUT YOUR OPERATION

Manufacturing managers, conferences, speeches, and books often get sidetracked on issues that, although interesting, are irrevelant to your operation. Discussions of these macroeconomic issues often include:

1. An analysis of the service sector versus the manufacturing sector of the economy. The results of this analysis range from the opinion that the service sector is supreme, to the conclu-

sion that the manufacturing sector is the driver of a nation's standard of living.

2. An analysis of the manufacturing productivity of various nations. The results here vary from the United States being in last place in the productivity race to the United States being in first place in the productivity race.

3. An analysis of the cost of labor from one nation to another. Once again, the conclusions reached on this point vary from one extreme to another.

4. The impacts of budget deficits, the valuation of the dollar, tax laws, trade policies, government regulations, and more. The number of opinions on these topics and the effect of these issues seem to be limited only by the number of authors in print. Certainly, no matter what you believe, there is at least one author who presents an acceptable position.

These issues are important, but they are not on the typical manufacturing manager's agenda. What is important to you is how to achieve winning manufacturing in your operation. You need to know the important, big-picture manufacturing issues, and then get on to the challenges you face with your operations. These issues are:

1. All great nations will have great manufacturing capabilities.
2. The United States is and always has been the overall leader in manufacturing productivity.
3. A discussion of direct labor costs from nation to nation is irrelevant.
4. It is important that a nation's government consists of people who understand the impact of their actions on manufacturing and the impact of manufacturing on their nation's well- being.

Similarly, it is easy to get sidetracked by dwelling on poor manufacturing management issues, such as:

1. Short-term orientation and results measurement;
2. Improper return on investment and accounting procedures to justify capital expenditures;
3. An orientation towards business acquisition instead of business building;
4. Poor implementation of technology;
5. Ineffective methods for dealing with unions; and
6. Poor development of manufacturing managers.

Once again, although these issues are important, being critical of past practices does not lead to improved operations. A focus on the past is not needed; an understanding of how to improve manufacturing is.

THIS IS A MANUFACTURING MANAGER'S BOOK

Manufacturing books are either management-focused or manufacturing-focused. The management-focused books, written to management people in manufacturing, emphasize the upper-echelon management issues, such as what products to produce, where to site plants, vertical integration, and so on. Manufacturing-focused books, written to manufacturing people in management, emphasize the improvement of manufacturing operations. *Winning Manufacturing* is a manufacturing-focused book.

Manufacturing books are either revolutionary or evolutionary. The revolutionary books believe manufacturing is a dirty, smelly, sweaty, dark world that repels quality personnel and espouse that a revolutionary program is needed to obtain manufacturing success. Evolutionary books are written with a total respect of the heritage of manufacturing and of the professionals who have brought manufacturing to its present state of development and argue that the only way to improve a manufacturing operation is via an evolutionary process. *Winning Manufacturing* is an evolutionary book.

Finally, manufacturing books are either general or specific. The general books present an interesting set of thought-provoking issues and a series of alternatives to consider. They argue in favor of developing a manufacturing strategic master plan, but do not explain the specific direction of manufacturing. The specific books present the direction of manufacturing upon which plans for improvement should be based. *Winning Manufacturing* is a specific book.

THIS BOOK IS ABOUT WINNING

Competitiveness is a fashionable term of the late 1980s. Books, magazines, and conferences focus on manufacturing competitiveness. This is unfortunate, because when companies adopt the stance that their objective is to strive to be competitive, they are inherently accepting the fact that another company is ahead of them and they must make significant progress just to be equal.

Many companies have been stung by the 'let's be competitive' bug, and they have focused on studying what others have done. In particular, Americans seem to be fixated on studying the Japanese. Of course, it is useful to understand your competition, your strengths, and your weaknesses, but it is a mistake to mimic what others have done.

I know of two companies that have hung red, yellow, and green traffic lights in their plants because a Japanese firm reportedly had success with that approach. Unfortunately, when asked the purpose of the traffic lights, the answers varied. Some thought the lights were part of a quality assurance program, some thought they had something to do with a performance measurement program, but most were unsure. So, even if the original traffic-light program was valid, mimicking of the program without truly understanding it resulted in another short-lived gimmick with no real substance.

It could have been worse. What would management have done if a highly respected Japanese firm was managed by a supervisor who was missing a leg? Would we require all supervisors to have one leg amputated?

It is naive to think that a company's future lies in duplicating what some other company has already done. Are you interested in competing with what your competition was doing last year, or do you want to win today? *Winning Manufacturing* is about winning today.

Often, the 'let's be competitive' bug makes a company's manufacturing management choke. Just like a basketball team can choke by believing that the other team is better, so too can a management team choke by dwelling on its inadequacies. Choking occurs when the fear of failure is stronger than the belief of winning. If a firm desires to be competitive, it will fear failure and often will choke. Thus, to be successful in manufacturing, we must put the whole concept of competitiveness out of our minds and instead, focus on the concept of winning manufacturing.

THE VALIDITY OF THIS BOOK WILL NOT CHANGE WITH TIME

Pursuing fads does not result in the long-term improvement of manufacturing and thus, is not a part of winning manufacturing. The only way to truly achieve winning manufacturing is to understand where manufacturing is headed. *Winning Manufacturing* explains the fundamental direction of manufacturing, a direction that will not change with time.

This book will not add another fad, gimmick, or program to manufacturing, but will define the approach that should be taken to continuously improve manufacturing.

THIS IS A HOW-TO BOOK

The objective of *Winning Manufacturing* is to help your company become a winning manufacturing company, but you will have to do more than just read this book. Improvements must be implemented in order for your company to become a winning manufacturing company. Each chapter of *Winning Manufacturing* concludes with a how-to section, and Chapter 22 presents the specific actions that are required to achieve winning manufacturing. If you follow the method given in this book, you will achieve winning manufacturing.

DYNAMIC CONSISTENCY

Winning manufacturing requires continuous change. Organizations have traditionally exhibited one of the following three attitudes towards change:

Type I Organizations:	Static Consistency
Type II Organizations:	Dynamic Inconsistency
Type III Organizations:	Dynamic Consistency

Type I organizations resist change. They pride themselves on maintaining the status quo and seldom realize there is an opportunity to improve. Type I managers believe—

1. "We have optimized our operations, and there is no room for improvement," or
2. "We have always been profitable, why should we change anything?"

Type I organizations are not compatible with winning manufacturing.

Type II organizations are dynamic, inconsistent organizations. They realize they are not successful and are actively installing new programs. They are busy organizations. Everyone is on a task force or two, but no one has a chance to work as the entire day is spent in meetings. There is no shared direction of where they are headed. Each person has his or her own manufacturing direction. Although there are islands of success, the whole of manufacturing is not improving. Manufacturing managers within Type II organizations are frustrated; the harder they work, the more they seem to lose. Type II organizations are actively pursuing manufacturing improvements and will benefit most from the process of winning manufacturing.

Type III organizations, however, truly understand the meaning of dynamic consistency. They are driven by an "improve, improve, improve" mentality based upon a consistent direction of manufacturing. Winning manufacturing organizations are Type III, dynamic, consistent organizations.

An example of a Type III organization is IBM, which believes in continuous improvement based upon what IBM founder, Thomas Watson, called the basic beliefs. At Dow Jones, the consistent company direction is referred to as the bedrocks, and at Toyota, this direction is referred to as philosophies of business. In winning manufacturing, the consistent direction is called Requirements of Success.

THE REQUIREMENTS OF SUCCESS FOR WINNING MANUFACTURING

The Requirements of Success for winning manufacturing are:

1. **Manufacturing Costs**. Manufacturing costs must be significantly reduced.
2. **Manufacturing and Marketing**. Manufacturing and marketing must become integrated and function as a team.
3. **Product Development**. Product development must become an integrated, iterative process.
4. **Global Marketplace**. All manufacturing decisions must be made within the context of an integrated global strategy.
5. **Lead Times**. Significant reductions in lead times must occur.
6. **Production Lot Sizes**. Production lot sizes and setup times must be reduced.
7. **Uncertainty**. All uncertainty must be minimized; discipline must be increased.
8. **Balance**. All manufacturing operations must be balanced.
9. **Production and Inventory Control**. The production and inventory control system must be straightforward and transparent.
10. **Inventories**. Drastic reductions in inventory must occur.
11. **Adaptability**. Manufacturing facilities, operations, and personnel must become more adaptable.
12. **Quality**. Product quality, vendor quality, and information quality must improve.
13. **Maintenance**. Manufacturing process failures must be minimized.
14. **Material Flow**. Material flow must be efficient.
15. **Material Tracking and Control**. Material tracking and control systems must be upgraded.
16. **Human Resources**. Every manager must be dedicated to creating an environment where every employee is motivated and happy.
17. **Team Players**. Everyone associated with manufacturing must work together as a team.

18. **Simplification**. All of manufacturing must be simplified.
19. **Integration**. All organizations and operations must be integrated.
20. **Understanding**. Manufacturing management must understand winning manufacturing.

HOW TO PURSUE WINNING MANUFACTURING

The process of winning manufacturing is presented in Figure 1 and explained in Table 2. Two important factors should be realized about this process:

1. It is a continuous process of improve, improve, improve.
2. It is anchored on a full, integrated understanding of all twenty Requirements of Success. Independent of which Requirements of Success are priorities, all twenty Requirements of Success must be embraced as the consistent direction of where manufacturing is headed.

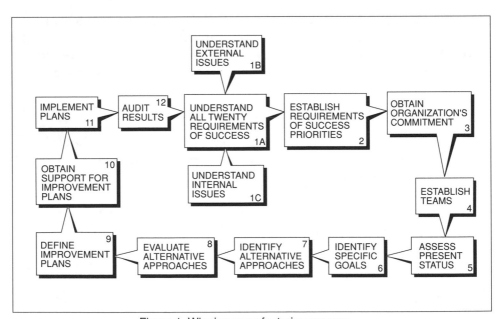

Figure 1. Winning manufacturing process

A winning basketball team is not the team that has the most desire to win, runs the fastest, jumps the highest, rebounds the best, shoots the best, plays the best defense, blocks the most shots, passes

TABLE 2
Explanation Of The Winning Manufacturing Process

STEP	FUNCTION	COMMENT
1a	Understand all twenty Requirements of Success	This requires an education program for all levels of an organization. Understanding all the Requirements of Success is the foundation for winning manufacturing.
1b	Understand external issues	This requires an external outreach via professional society involvement, participation in trade shows, seminars and conferences and reading of magazines and books. A coordinated effort is required if external issues are to be well understood.
1c	Understand internal issues	A winning manufacturing organization must understand the mission, resources, constraints and objectives of their overall organization. A prerequisite of winning manufacturing is understanding a company's business plan.
2	Establish Requirements of Success priorities	To implement improvements, an organization must have focus. This step requires that management determine which Requirements of Success offer the greatest opportunity for improvement.
3	Obtain organizational commitment	Management must make a clear commitment to implement the justified improvements for the prioritized Requirements of Success. This commitment must be uncompromised.
4	Establish teams	A team having a broad-based representation and the ability to make decisions should be established for each prioritized Requirement of Success. This team must be action-oriented.
5	Assess present status	This assessment will result in the baseline against which improvements will be measured. Both quantitative and qualitative factors should be assessed.
6	Identify specific goals	The identification of clear, measurable, time-related goals for each prioritized Requirement of Success. For example, the reduction of raw material inventory to $300,000 by June 1.
7	Identify alternative approaches	The creative process of identifying alternative systems, procedures, equipment or methods to achieve the specified goals. The investigation of all feasible alternatives.
8	Evaluate alternative approaches	The economic and qualitative evaluation of the identified alternatives. The economic evaluation should adhere to corporate guidelines while estimating the full economic benefit of pursuing each alternative.
9	Define improvement plans	Based upon the evaluation done in Step 8, select the best approach. Define a detailed implementation and cash flow schedule.
10	Obtain support for improvement plans	Sell the improvement plans to management. Document the alternatives, the evaluation and the justification. Help management visualize the improved operation.
11	Implement plans	Oversee development, installation, soft load, start-up and debug. Train operators and assure proper systems utilization. Stay with effort until results are achieved.
12	Audit results	Document actual systems operation. Compare results with the specified goal and anticipated performance. Identify and document discrepancies. Provide appropriate feedback.

the best, hustles the most, or dribbles the best. A winning basketball team is the team that does all of these things well. Similarly with winning manufacturing, all twenty Requirements of Success must be pursued.

Each cycle of the winning manufacturing process begins with Step 1, which has three distinct tasks: understanding all twenty Requirements of Success (Step 1a), understanding external issues (Step 1b), and understanding internal issues (Step 1c).

Understanding external issues (Step 1b) requires an awareness of factors outside of your organization that have an impact on your organization. Factors such as shifts in the marketplace, availability of new technology, actions taken by competitors, and government regulations will play important roles in the winning manufacturing process. Without this continuous external scanning, an organization becomes self-centered and loses touch with reality. Once this happens, organizations have difficulty establishing priorities. Poor priority setting results in organizations doing the wrong things more efficiently. This is not winning manufacturing.

Understanding internal issues (Step 1c) requires an awareness of your organization's business plan. Manufacturing management should be intimately involved with your company's business planning process and should establish the priorities for winning manufacturing within the context of the organization's business plan. It is only by tying the manufacturing improvement process to the overall business plan that winning manufacturing can be achieved.

Step 2 of the winning manufacturing process (establish Requirements of Success priorities) requires the completion of the manufacturing management priorities questionnaire (Figure 2) and a winning manufacturing prioritization meeting (see Appendix C). The questionnaire should be completed by all manufacturing managers who understand the twenty Requirements of Success. The questionnaires should be summarized and used as a starting point for the meeting. It is not unusual for there to be significant differences of opinion as to which Requirements of Success are priorities. The objective of the meeting is to reach a consensus on which five to seven Requirements of Success should be the focus for the next winning manufacturing improvement cycle.

Once the prioritized Requirements of Success are established, a series of meetings should be conducted with the employees most affected by each prioritized requirement to obtain the organization's commitment (Step 3) and understanding of the prioritized requirements. These meeting are called winning manufacturing Requirements of Success initiation meetings (see Appendix D). Based upon the input received at these initiation meetings, a team should be

1. OUT OF A TOTAL OF 100 POINTS, RATE THE IMPORTANCE OF PURSUING THE FOLLOW-
ING REQUIREMENTS OF SUCCESS (THE HIGHER THE POINTS ASSIGNED, THE GREATER
THE IMPORTANCE).

REQUIREMENTS OF SUCCESS	POINTS
A. MANUFACTURING COSTS	
B. MANUFACTURING AND MARKETING	
C. PRODUCT DEVELOPMENT	
D. GLOBAL MARKETPLACE	
E. LEAD TIMES	
F. PRODUCTION LOT SIZES	
G. UNCERTAINTY	
H. BALANCE	
I. PRODUCTION AND INVENTORY CONTROL	
J. INVENTORIES	
K. ADAPTABILITY	
L. QUALITY	
M. MAINTENANCE	
N. MATERIAL FLOW	
O. MATERIAL TRACKING AND CONTROL	
P. HUMAN RESOURCES	
Q. TEAM PLAYERS	
R. SIMPLIFICATION	
S. INTEGRATION	
T. UNDERSTANDING	
TOTAL	100

2. STATE THE GOAL THAT YOU THINK SHOULD BE ESTABLISHED FOR THE FIVE HIGHEST-
PRIORITY REQUIREMENTS OF SUCCESS.

REQUIREMENTS OF SUCCESS	GOAL
1.	
2.	
3.	
4.	
5.	

Figure 2. Manufacturing management priorities questionnaire

established (Step 4) for each prioritized Requirement of Success. These teams should complete the first cycle (Steps 5 through 12) by following the how-to descriptions at the end of each chapter.

At the end of each winning manufacturing improvement cycle, the cycle should begin again with Step 1. The result will be continuous improvement.

The next step is to read this book. Through understanding the material presented here, you will be able to contribute to your company's pursuit of winning manufacturing.

REFERENCES

Avishai, B. 1989. A CEO's common sense of CIM: an interview with J. Tracey O'Rourke. *Harvard Business Review*. January-February. Vol. 67, no. 1.

Brownstein, V. 1987. Crawling out of the trade tunnel. *Fortune*. December 21. Vol. 116, no. 14.

Chipello, C.J. 1988. Many U.S. plants lag in automation, new study finds. *Wall Street Journal*. October 14.

Crosby, P.B. 1979. *Quality Is Free*. New American Library. New York.

DeGeus, A.P. 1988. Planning as learning. *Harvard Business Review*. March-April. Vol. 66, no. 2.

Drucker, P.F. 1980. *Managing In Turbulent Times*. Harper & Row. New York.

Groover, M.P. 1980. *Automation, Production Systems and Computer-Aided Manufacturing*. Prentice-Hall. Englewood Cliffs, New Jersey.

Gunn, T.G. 1987. *Manufacturing for Competitive Advantage: Becoming a World Class Manufacturer*. Ballinger Publishing Company. Cambridge, Massachusetts.

Harrington, J.J. 1984. *Understanding the Manufacturing Process*. Marcel Decker, Inc. New York.

Hayes, R.H., and Wheelwright, S.C. 1984. *Restoring Our Competitive Edge: Competing Through Manufacturing*. John Wiley & Sons. New York.

Huber, R.F. 1987. Today, it takes more to be competitive. *Production*. December.Vol. 99, no. 12.

McGill, M.F. 1988. *American Business and the Quick Fix*. Henry Holt. New York.

Naisbitt, J., and Aburdene, P. 1985. *Reinventing the Corporation: Transforming Your Job and Your Company for the New Information Society*. Warner Books. New York.

Naldish, N.L. 1988. Are you planning in the dark? *Manufacturing Engineering*. July. Vol. 101, no. 1.

Nasar, S. 1988. America's competitive revival. *Fortune*. January 4.Vol. 117, no. 1.

Ouchi, W. 1981. *Theory Z*. Addison-Wesley. Reading, Massachusetts.

Peters, T.J., and Austin, N. 1985. *A Passion For Excellence*. Random House. New York.

Peters, T.J., and Waterman, R.H. 1985. *In Search of Excellence*. Random House. New York.

Porter, M.E. 1985. *Competitive Advantage*. Free Press. New York.

Schonberger, R. 1982. *Japanese Manufacturing Techniques*. Free Press. New York.

_____. 1986. *World Class Manufacturing*. The Free Press. New York.

Skinner, W. 1985. *Manufacturing: The Formidable Competitive Weapon*. John Wiley & Sons. New York.

Tompkins, J.A. 1986. NEA: The answer to manufacturing automation excellence. *Industrial Product Bulletin*. January. Vol. 43, no. 1.

_____. 1986. Technology fear. *Industrial Product Bulletin*. September. Vol. 43, no. 8.

Chapter 2
MANUFACTURING COSTS

MANUFACTURING COSTS MUST BE SIGNIFICANTLY REDUCED.

Winning manufacturing requires significant manufacturing cost reductions. The Type I, Type II, and Type III organizations described in Chapter 1 take the same approaches to manufacturing cost reduction as they do toward change.

Type I organizations set a goal of reducing costs by a couple of percentage points per year. This approach results in a wide variety of limited-scope, cost-cutting measures. Examples of these limited-scope activities follow:

1. Consolidation of forms to eliminate excess paper work,
2. Relayout of work stations to minimize operator walking,
3. Redesign of shipping cartons to reduce the cost of packaging materials,
4. Installation of load detectors on conveyors to save energy, and
5. Recycling of scrap material to minimize waste.

The real objective of these limited-scope activities is cost containment, not significant cost reduction. This is not winning manufacturing.

Type II organizations set a goal of improving one specific factor (inventory reduction, increased quality, or increased productivity) and pursue this goal independently of the overall direction of manufacturing. The cost reduction achieved for the targeted factor is often accompanied by cost increases in other factors. This is not winning manufacturing.

Type III organizations believe in continuous manufacturing cost reductions that are consistent with the overall direction of manufacturing. Type III organizations believe that today's optimal solution is just one step in the continuous process of improve, improve, improve! Winning manufacturing is based upon a day-by-day, step-by-step, dynamic, never-ending continuum of cost reductions. Today's great operation is next week's good operation, which is next month's average operation, which is next quarter's poor operation. In winning manufacturing organizations, the cost reduction process is one of never-ending improvement.

THE MAGNITUDE OF SIGNIFICANT MANUFACTURING COST REDUCTIONS

The percentage reduction in manufacturing costs that would be considered significant for your organization depends upon your industry and your company's progress. However, significant cost reduction is not a 2 percent, a 5 percent, or even a 10 percent reduction in manufacturing cost. Winning manufacturing requires a reduction of 40 percent to 60 percent.

The Requirement of Success to significantly reduce the costs of manufacturing may seem routine, but once you understand what is meant by significant, manufacturing cost reduction is put in a different light. The attitude and approach of someone attempting to reduce the costs of manufacturing by five percent is totally different from the attitude and approach of someone attempting a 50 percent reduction.

Significant reductions in the manufacturing costs will result in closed plants and fewer employees. These events are the natural result of winning manufacturing. Plant closings are always a major news story, but when an industry's production capacity exceeds demand, traditional manufacturing plants will either have to be operated at low levels of utilization or be closed.

For example, world automotive demand is estimated at 30 million to 35 million vehicles per year. Production capacity is estimated at 40 million to 45 million vehicles per year. Even though demand will increase, capacity will increase even faster. In North America, annual demand for vehicles is roughly 12 million, but capacity by 1993 will exceed 18 million vehicles. At least five, and maybe as many as ten, North American automotive assembly plants will have to close between 1990 and 1994. During the same period, ten to twenty worldwide automotive assembly plants will have to close. Likewise, plant closings in the steel, heavy equipment, textiles, and computer industries are forthcoming. Plant closings are a natural result of certain firms having a dynamic, consistent direction for winning manufacturing and reducing costs. Traditional manufacturing plants overprice their products, lose market share, and eventually have no choice but to close.

In 1919, almost 40 percent of all nonfarm workers in the United States worked in manufacturing. By 1950, this number dropped to 34 percent, and by 1965 it was 30 percent. Today, only 20 percent of the nonfarm workers are employed in manufacturing. This trend has resulted in the erroneous belief that we are now living in a post-industrial service economy; an information society. The fact that over this same time (1919-1989), manufacturing has maintained approximately 24 percent of the Gross Domestic Product totally refutes the claim that our industrial economy is dying. The truth is we are living in a dynamic industrial economy where significant cost reductions in manufacturing result in greater overall output with fewer total people employed.

TODAY'S MANUFACTURING COSTS

Today's manufacturing costs consist of direct labor, materials, and overhead. Although the definitions of these items differ from company to company and manufacturing costs vary from industry to industry, they share similarities:

1. Direct labor is a small portion of the total manufacturing cost.
2. Materials costs and overhead costs are roughly of equal importance to the manufacturing costs.

Direct labor costs vary from 5 percent to 15 percent of the total costs of manufacturing; materials and overhead vary from 35 percent to 55 percent of the total.

Figure 3 illustrates manufacturing costs and how the efforts of manufacturing cost reduction are typically allocated, by overemphasizing direct labor and underemphasizing overhead. The amount of effort allocated to manufacturing cost reduction should be proportional to the costs of manufacturing. For example, if direct labor is 10 percent of the total cost of manufacturing, then 10 percent of the cost reduction effort should focus on direct labor. Similarly, if materials and overhead are each 45 percent of the total cost of manufacturing, then 45 percent of the cost reduction efforts should be spent on each of these cost components.

HOW TO SIGNIFICANTLY REDUCE THE COSTS OF MANUFACTURING

Winning manufacturers will significantly reduce manufacturing costs through quality leadership that must raise the expectations and the aspirations of the organization. The leadership must stress that dynamic operations based upon the consistent direction of manufacturing is expected and should be pursued.

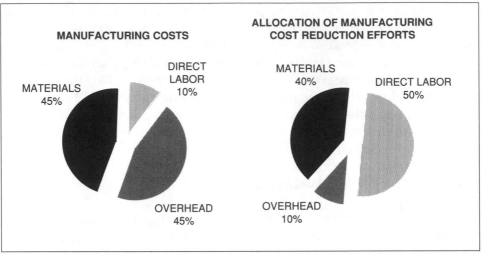

Figure 3. Manufacturing costs and allocation of cost reduction efforts

The first step to significant manufacturing cost reduction is to document the present costs of manufacturing. This documentation must accurately and precisely define and detail the costs of manufacturing. Often, this can reveal cost reduction opportunities. For example:

1. What percentage of the total manufacturing cost is direct labor? material? and overhead?
2. What costs are included in overhead? Are these overhead costs fixed or variable, and are these costs fairly allocated?
3. How are inventory carrying costs considered? Are these costs properly allocated?
4. Are there costs buried in overhead that would more accurately be allocated to materials (for example, packaging materials)?
5. How are material yield, salvage, and waste costs allocated?
6. Why do material losses occur?
7. How is rework handled? Does this properly reflect the actual cost allocation?
8. How is overtime handled? Is this done properly?
9. What are the definitions of direct and indirect labor? Can indirect labor be allocated directly to certain products?
10. Are general factory expenses (energy, taxes, insurance, maintenance, and space costs) properly allocated?

Once the details of the present manufacturing costs are well understood, specific manufacturing cost reduction goals should be established and communicated throughout the organization. Broad-based staff participation should be encouraged.

A wide range of alternatives for each cost reduction goal should be considered. Many of the alternatives will focus on one of the other nineteen Requirements of Success. In these situations, consult the how-to sections at the end of the appropriate chapters. The alternatives should be economically and qualitatively analyzed; the justifiable ones should be translated into an improvement plan that is sold to management and implemented. The last step of each cost reduction effort should be an audit of the implemented performance to the anticipated performance. Corrective action should be taken when necessary.

REFERENCES

Chew, W.B. 1988. No nonsense guide to measuring productivity. *Harvard Business Review*. January-February. Vol. 66, No. 1.

Cohen, S.S., and Zysman, J. 1987. *Manufacturing Matters: The Myth of the Post-Industrial Economy*. Basic Books. New York.

Gunn, T.G. 1987. *Manufacturing for Competitive Advantage: Becoming a World Class Manufacturer*. Ballinger Publishing Company. Cambridge, Massachusetts.

Hayes, R.H., and Wheelwright, S.C. 1984. *Restoring Our Competitive Edge: Competing Through Manufacturing*. John Wiley & Sons. New York.

Huber, R.F. 1987. A prophetic warning. *Production*. November. Vol. 99, No. 11.

Mehltretter, G.W. Jr. 1988. Reducing unit cost. *Turnaround Management Association Newsletter*. Research Triangle Park, North Carolina. September.

Naisbitt, J. 1981. *Megatrends*. Warner Books. New York.

Porter, M.E. 1985. *Competitive Advantage*. Free Press. New York.

Tompkins, J.A. 1987. Optimality attitudes vs. incremental improvement attitudes. *Industrial Product Bulletin*. July. Vol. 44, no. 7.

Winter, R.E. 1985. U.S. manufacturing: it's alive and well. *The Wall Street Journal*. December 23.

_____ 1987. Glutted markets, a global overcapacity hurts many industries; no easy cure seen. *The Wall Street Journal*. March 9.

_____ 1988. Study of car industry sees plant closing over next five years. *The Wall Street Journal*. February 8.

Chapter 3
MANUFACTURING AND MARKETING

MANUFACTURING AND MARKETING MUST BECOME INTEGRATED AND FUNCTION AS A TEAM.

Winning manufacturing cannot be achieved at the expense of another team player. It must include the reality that manufacturing cannot truly win unless all functions associated with manufacturing also win. Two organizational functions that have been at war since the 1950s are manufacturing and marketing. If your organization does not have winning marketing, you cannot have winning manufacturing.

The relationship between manufacturing and marketing is essential; you cannot have winning manufacturing if you do not know—

1. What the customer desires,
2. What to produce,
3. How much to produce,
4. How to package, label, and ship, and
5. When to ship.

A positive teamwork relationship between manufacturing and marketing, can be built in three phases:

Phase I: Cease-Fire
Phase II: Peace
Phase III: Synergism

PHASE I: CEASE-FIRE

The first critical step in establishing a positive teamwork relationship between manufacturing and marketing is to call a truce between the two sides. As long as the war between your manufacturing organization and your marketing organization continues, there will be no winning manufacturing. The cease-fire must be mandated and led by upper management and will be made permanent only after each side understands the other's perspective. Only when mutual understanding truly exists is there hope for peace (Phase II). Manufacturing and marketing will not be easily molded into a team. The difficulty of this task depends upon the magnitude of the manufacturing-marketing war.

Table 3 presents a stereotypical view of how manufacturing and marketing see the manufacturing-marketing war. Given these views, it is not surprising that manufacturing and marketing require external assistance to achieve a cease-fire. The cease-fire should be mandated as follows:

Step 1. Upper management sends a memo to the appropriate manufacturing and marketing managers. A copy of Table 3 should be attached to this memo. The memo explains winning manufacturing and requests that manufacturing and marketing each prepare the equivalent of Table 3 for their specific company.

Step 2. Send manufacturing's view to marketing and marketing's view to manufacturing. Upper management should review the stereotypical view, the manufacturing view, and the marketing view. Upper management should then identify problems, conflicts, and misunderstandings; establish an agenda to resolve these misunderstandings; and arrange a meeting.

Step 3. Upper management initiates the meeting with a description of winning manufacturing and then states that the stereotypical views presented in Table 3 will not be accepted within the company. Each of the identified problems, conflicts, and misunderstandings should be discussed. A positive version of Table 3 entitled "The XYZ Company's View of Manufacturing and Marketing Relationships" should be developed at the meeting.

Step 4. Upper management publishes the chart developed in Step 3 and declares the cease-fire. Upper management has now laid the groundwork for peace (Phase II) and for synergism (Phase III).

PHASE II: PEACE

Although upper management can dictate the cease-fire, they cannot dictate peace. Peace can only be obtained by communication between manufacturing and marketing. Although the cease-fire can be obtained via a few memos and meetings, peace cannot be obtained as easily. It can only be obtained by an ongoing, long-term commitment to work in unison that will only be obtained once manufacturing and marketing understand that their individual successes are tied to mutual success. Either manufacturing and marketing both win, or they both lose.

In order for the process to work, the commitment must be consistent and the communications must be dynamic. Manufacturing and marketing must continuously communicate on issues, such as customization, customer expectations, and forecasts.

TABLE 3
A Stereotypic View Of The Manufacturing/Marketing War

WHAT MANUFACTURING BELIEVES ABOUT MARKETING	WHAT MARKETING BELIEVES ABOUT MARKETING
Marketing desires low-cost, high-quality, instantaneous delivery and unlimited options even though the marketing forecasts are inaccurate. In general, marketing people are uninformed and don't actually understand the reality of business.	Marketing is in touch with the ever-changing, unpredictable desires of the marketplace and has a true understanding of how to make the company successful. Marketing has positioned the company very well in the marketplace in spite of the lack of support from manufacturing.
WHAT MANUFACTURING BELIEVES ABOUT MANUFACTURING	**WHAT MARKETING BELIEVES ABOUT MANUFACTURING**
Manufacturing has done a tremendous job of working with too little capital in creating a manufacturing machine that, given the proper notification, can respond to any reasonable production schedule. Manufacturing produces products at a quality level, consistent with their design and at a minimal cost.	Manufacturing would like to run the same product, without any changes, forever, and still would not be able to produce at a quality or cost level that would satisfy the customer. In general, manufacturing people are lazy, unimaginative, and really don't care about the changing needs of the marketplace.

Customization

As customers become more sophisticated, they demand a higher level of product customization. The number of options available to customers will continue to increase, and winning manufacturing must have the ability to respond to this customization requirement. Winning manufacturing thus must provide a flexible manufacturing capability.

Manufacturing and marketing must communicate on the customers' desires and the costs of various product options. Marketing must help manufacturing understand the customers' desires, and manufacturing must help marketing understand the envelope of customization that can be handled economically.

Customer Expectations

Marketing must define the customers' true desires and needs to manufacturing. The meaning of high-quality, high-reliability products must be specified for the marketing niche. A clear, easily understood, measurable definition of the level of quality and reliability that the customer expects for the price being paid for the product is vital. For example, the quality and reliability expectations of a customer who purchases a $10,000 Rolex watch are different from the quality and reliability expectations of a customer who purchases a $25 Timex watch.

Likewise, marketing must fairly define the customer service expectations of response time, order sizes, order frequency, packaging requirements, product and package labeling, order audit trails and shipping modes. Manufacturing and marketing must clearly understand the expectations so that the realistic customer expectations can be achieved economically.

Forecasts

Manufacturing must understand that they will never receive an accurate forecast; however, manufacturing deserves to understand the level of accuracy they should expect from the forecast. That is, if the forecast is for eight parts, is that eight with a range of zero to twenty or eight with a range of seven to nine?

Marketing must understand the actions manufacturing takes based on the forecasts and take responsibility for communicating forecast changes according to a predefined schedule and level of accuracy. Manufacturing and marketing must work together not only on these short-term production scheduling issues, but also on the long-term capacity forecasts.

Marketing must understand the effect that end-of-month, end-of-quarter, end-of-year order flurries have on manufacturing, and establish procedures to smooth production requirements. Marketing must accept the responsibility of coordinating promotions and special sales programs with manufacturing to ensure that these programs can be realistically and economically handled. New product or new option start-ups require considerable cooperation between manufacturing and marketing, and a new product introduction should be planned only when a mutually agreeable schedule has been established.

The winning vision of manufacturing requires that manufacturing and marketing work as a team to coordinate all forecasts so that, to the greatest extent possible, the forecast becomes a prediction of what actually will occur.

PHASE III: SYNERGISM

The result of Phase I, is that manufacturing and marketing stop fighting. The result of Phase II, is that manufacturing and marketing work together. The result of Phase III goes beyond working together. In this phase, manufacturing and marketing become integrated, and the synergistic benefits of winning manufacturing become a reality.

Once winning manufacturing is in place, the following will occur:

1. The past restrictions on marketing will be removed, and marketing will be able to position the product so that more units will be sold.
2. Because more units will be sold, the expansion of winning manufacturing will be required and investment in improved flexible manufacturing facilities will take place.
3. Because improved flexible manufacturing facilities will exist, smaller lot sizes, more customization, and increased quality will result.
4. Because smaller lots will be produced, inventories will be reduced and customer service will be improved.
5. Because inventories will be reduced, manufacturing costs will decrease and this will result in further increases in the quantity of units that can be sold.
6. Because customer service will improve, further increases will occur in the quantity of units that can be sold.
7. Because of increased quality, the manufacturing costs will further decrease and thus, once again, the number of units that can be sold will increase.

This discussion becomes quite clear when illustrated (see Figure 4). The synergy between manufacturing and marketing continues on an upward spiral of increased sales, enhanced winning manufacturing, increased sales, enhanced winning manufacturing, increased sales, enhanced winning manufacturing, and so on.

Once winning manufacturing is in place, the synergistic benefits of an integrated manufacturing and marketing team will be perpetuated and escalated.

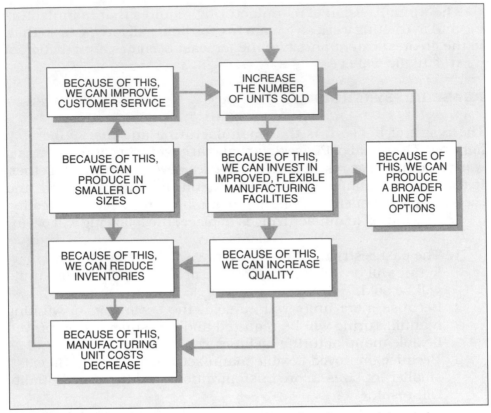

Figure 4. Synergistic benefit of winning manufacturing on an integrated
manufacturing-marketing team

HOW TO INTEGRATE MANUFACTURING AND MARKETING

Manufacturing and marketing will become integrated and function
as a team only after upper management mandates that this will
occur. Upper management must provide the leadership and the determination for manufacturing and marketing to establish a positive
teamwork relationship. The approach that should be taken by upper
management to create this team should be done in phases. Phase I
(Cease-Fire) creates understanding, Phase II (Peace) creates communications, and Phase III (Synergy) results in winning manufacturing
and winning marketing.

REFERENCES

Gunn, T.G. 1987. *Manufacturing for Competitive Advantage: Becoming a World Class Manufacturer.* Ballinger Publishing Company. Cambridge, Massachusetts.

Hayes, R.H., and Wheelwright, S.C. 1984. *Restoring Our Competitive Edge: Competing Through Manufacturing.* John Wiley & Sons. New York.

Waterman, R.H. 1987. *The Renewal Factor: How the Best Get and Keep the Competitive Edge.* Bantam Books. New York.

Chapter 4
PRODUCT DEVELOPMENT

PRODUCT DEVELOPMENT MUST BECOME AN INTEGRATED, ITERATIVE PROCESS.

The critical relationship between manufacturing and marketing presented in Chapter 3 is expanded here to explain how, based upon the manufacturing and marketing synergy, the foundation for long-term, winning manufacturing is established.

Essential to winning manufacturing is integrated, iterative product development. Product development *is not* market analysis, product design, process design, manufacturing systems design, or procurement specifications. Product development *is* the interactive process whereby the customer, marketing, sales, product designers, process designers, purchasing, vendors, and manufacturing work together to develop a product that meets customers' expectations and can be manufactured economically.

TRADITIONAL PRODUCT DEVELOPMENT

The traditional product development process, exemplified by the automotive industry, has occurred in many industries and is best described as 'throwing it over the wall.' This sequential process is illustrated in Figure 5.

Between each pair of functions in Figure 5 is a tall, thick, solid wall. Each function believes the functions before it are incompetent. The process is not only sequential, but also walled into separate product development functions.

Thus, when marketing throws the product goals over the wall to the product designers, the designers believe the goals are unrealistic and lack a clear understanding of available technology. The designers alter the goals and design a product to meet the corrected market analysis. Product design then throws the design over the wall to both the process designers and purchasing.

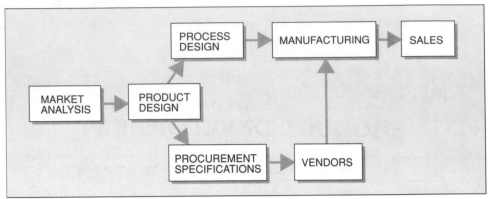

Figure 5. Traditional product development

Because of what has been submitted to them, the process designers believe the product designers lack an understanding of the real world. The process designers find holes that are not aligned, parts that cannot be manufactured, components that will not fit together, and other design flaws. Therefore, they have no choice but to correct the product design so that it can be manufactured. Because the process designers have to start all over on product design, they find themselves running into scheduling problems. Without having enough time to check their work, they then throw the process sheets over the wall to manufacturing. Similarly, the interaction between purchasing and the vendors indicates that the product design is flawed. Procurement works with the vendors to correct the product design. Once the redesign is completed, the vendors are placed under contract to produce what is really needed for the product to be produced economically.

Manufacturing then receives process sheets and components that must be corrected before they can be implemented. In fact, manufacturing often goes back and changes the original market analysis, which affects the product design, which in turn forces change in the process design. Manufacturing is short on time, so they hurry into production while still designing the process. Thus, manufacturing is only able to produce the first products by flooding the floor with product modifications, engineering change orders, and quick fixes to make the process work.

After the first few products are produced, they are thrown over the wall to sales, which also receives a suggested sales price and a quarterly sales forecast. Sales is not happy with what they have been asked to sell and are certain they are the only people in the company who have any awareness of the customer. They don't see how they can be asked to sell such a substandard product. The sales group then creates sufficient noise to initiate an investigation as to how they could be given such a substandard product to sell.

As the investigation crawls back over all the walls, the results in each room are either:

1. "We are not responsible for this product as unrealistic requirements were dictated to us. We did all that could be done to get this product on track." or
2. "We are not responsible for this product as our work has been changed. The final product is not what we recommended."

This review of product development by throwing it over the wall leads to the following conclusions:

1. Although, in theory, the market analysis records the customer's needs and wants, the customer is not really a part of the traditional product development process. It is not surprising, therefore, that a product does not meet the customer's needs or wants.
2. Little or no feedback occurs across the walls. This results in added resentment among the various groups.
3. No one is accountable for the results of the product development process. The end product was developed by either the other group or no one.
4. The length of time from the market analysis to the sale of the first unit is so long that the market analysis is often no longer valid. At each phase of the product development process, the entire product development process is restarted. This duplication is expensive and time consuming.

In summary, the traditional product development process does not work. Winning manufacturing requires a significantly streamlined, integrated, interactive product development process.

PRODUCT DEVELOPMENT PROGRAMS

Table 1 documents several product development programs pursued in the 1980s. Table 4 describes several of them.

Beginning with the traditional throw it over the wall approach, each of the product development programs has progressively enhanced the process. Winning manufacturing product development, therefore, is the culmination of these product development programs. Figure 6 illustrates this evolution.

WINNING MANUFACTURING PRODUCT DEVELOPMENT

Figure 7 illustrates the time span from product conception to product availability for both traditional and winning manufacturing product development; product development for winning manufacturing requires less than 50 percent of the time required for traditional product development. For example, at AT&T, the product development time for telephones has been reduced from two years to one year; at Navistar, the product development for trucks has been reduced from five years to two-and-one-half years; at Hewlett-Packard, the product development time for computer printers has been reduced from 54 months to 22 months. Because of the tremendous amount of interactions, however, the time spent by marketing, product design, sales, process design and procurement on winning manufacturing product development is more than the time spent on traditional product development. Consequently, the cost of winning manufacturing product development is greater than the cost of traditional product development.

TABLE 4
Product Development Programs Defined

PROGRAMS	DEFINITION
Group Technology	A design and manufacturing technique where the similarity of components is exploited to simplify the design and manufacturing process. New components are designed in the context of existing families of similar components to reduce duplication of design efforts.
Value Analysis	The analysis of the functions provided by a product to the cost of providing the function, with the objective of maximizing the functions received per unit of cost.
Failure Mode and Effects Analysis	A systematic study of the causes and effects of product failures. The minimization of failure by redesigning the product to eliminate the cause for the failure.
Taguchi Methods	The identification of the product design parameters that must be controlled in manufacturing to assure quality production. A method of relating product variability to quality losses and therefore, a technique to determine what level of variability should be economically allowed for a product.
Simultaneous Engineering	Also known as concurrent engineering or process-driven design. The performance of product design and process design in parallel. Considerable interaction between product and process design to assure the product is designed to be easily manufactured.
Design for Manufacture (DFM)	Also known as integrated engineering. The integration of product design and process design into one group to simplify the manufacturing of components. Instead of having product and process design groups working together as in simultaneous engineering, the groups are combined into one group.
Design for Assembly	A step beyond DFM in that now DFM is done for all components and how the components may be assembled.
Mechatronics	The word originally came from the application of automation to the integration of mechanical and electronic engineering. A multidisciplined, integrated approach to product development to facilitate automated manufacturing.

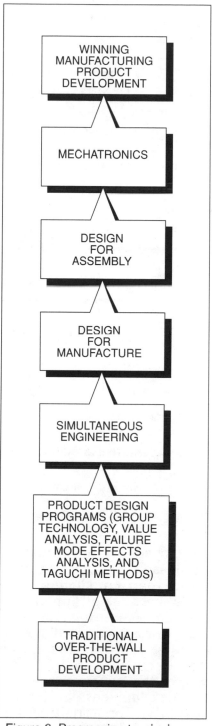

Figure 6. Progression to winning
manufacturing product
development

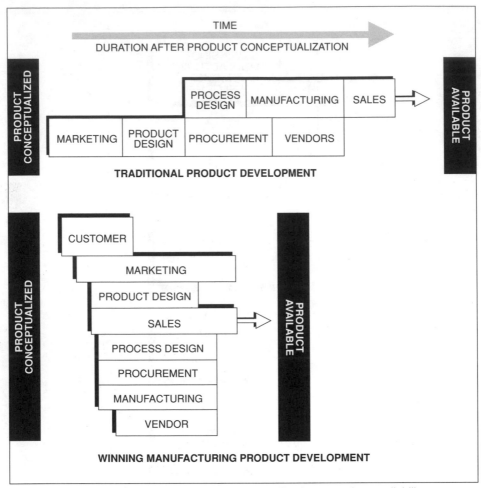

Figure 7. Duration from product conceptualization to product availability

A product developed by the winning manufacturing process, however, will cost less to manufacture and achieve better performance and acceptance than a product that results from the traditional process. Moreover, because all functions are working simultaneously, the winning manufacturing product development process will be quicker. Thus, your company will have greater control over your marketplace. Because you respond quicker, your competition is on the defensive.

Table 5 compares the issues for traditional and winning manufacturing product development. In brief, winning manufacturing product development is preferred, because a better, lower-cost product is brought to market sooner.

Figure 8 presents the process of winning manufacturing product development. The comparison of Figures 8 and 5 illustrate that winning manufacturing product development is integrated and iterative, while traditional product development is separate and sequential. In winning manufacturing product development, each element is done in the context of, and in communication with, the other elements.

TABLE 5
Winning Manufacturing And Traditional Product Development Compared

WINNING MANUFACTURING PRODUCT DEVELOPMENT	TRADITIONAL PRODUCT DEVELOPMENT
Faster to market	Slower to market
More manhours in product development	Fewer manhours in product development
More expensive product development	Less expensive product development
Less manufacturing cost	More manufacturing cost
Superior product performance	Inferior product performance
Superior product acceptance by marketplace	Inferior product acceptance by marketplace
Preferred approach	Obsolete approach

Figure 8 should be viewed in conjunction with Table 6, which provides a condensed explanation of each of the links in Figure 8. In brief, the customer, marketing, sales, product design, process de-

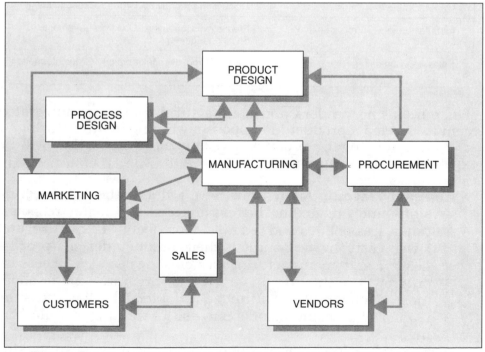

Figure 8. The functional interactions of winning manufacturing product development

TABLE 6
Winning Manufacturing Product Development Explained

LINK	EXPLANATION
Customer <–> Marketing	Customer needs and wants. Customization. Forecasts.
Marketing <–> Sales	Definition of product objectives. Customization. Sales objectives.
Marketing <–> Product Design	Definition of product objectives. Customization. Refinement of product design.
Product Design <–> Process Design	Manufacturing of the product. Product design. Customization.
Product Design <–> Manufacturing	Manufacturability of the product. Make/buy decisions. Product design.
Process Design <–> Manufacturing	Manufacturability of the product. Production routing. Production methods.
Product Design <–> Procurement	Manufacturability of the purchased components. Make/buy decisions. Refinement of product design.
Marketing <–> Manufacturing	Refinement of product objectives. Forecasts. Customization.
Procurement <–> Vendors	Manufacturability of the purchased components. Production forecasts and schedules. Quality requirements.
Manufacturing <–> Vendors	Purchased components. Shipment scheduling.
Manufacturing <–> Sales	Production scheduling. Orders. Order status.
Manufacturing <–> Procurement	Production scheduling. Quality requirements. Shipping requirements.
Sales <–> Customers	Orders. Production information. Order information.

sign, purchasing, vendors, and manufacturing work as an integrated team to develop a product in support of winning manufacturing.

Four issues of the product development process that will be explored in later chapters are:

1. **Team Players**. Many firms have reduced their engineering staffs and are finding increased efficiency, faster response times, less politics and red tape, more focused expertise, and lower costs by outsourcing their product design, process design, and manufacturing systems design. A necessary outgrowth of this trend is a need for organizations to adopt more of a team-player attitude. (Chapter 18 will address the team player Requirement of Success for winning manufacturing.)

2. **Simplification**. Simplification is a critical factor in making

winning manufacturing product development a reality. Product development simplification reduces the number of parts in a product. As the number of parts is reduced, the entire product development process is streamlined. As the number of parts is reduced, it is easier to maintain product quality and to reduce the costs of manufacturing. (Chapter 19 will address the simplification Requirement of Success for winning manufacturing.)

3. **Integration**. Integration of various organizational elements and even vendors is a requirement of winning manufacturing product development. To facilitate this process, computer-aided design (CAD), computer-aided engineering (CAE), and electronic data interchange (EDI) are important design/communication tools. (Chapter 20 will address the application of these tools and the role of the integration Requirement of Success for winning manufacturing.)

4. **Understanding**. An important aspect of economic manufacturing is manufacturing's understanding of the envelope within which they operate. This envelope must be sufficiently flexible to allow the production of a significant variety of, as yet, undefined products. Manufacturing must understand its mission and establish a set of manufacturing standards that will guide product development. (Chapter 21 will address the understanding Requirement of Success for winning manufacturing.)

HOW TO ESTABLISH AN INTEGRATED, ITERATIVE PRODUCT DEVELOPMENT PROCESS

The most successful illustration of a completed winning manufacturing product development project is the Ford Motor Company's Team Taurus. The approach Ford has taken to winning manufacturing product development is the same approach you should take: winning manufacturing product development should be implemented on a product-by-product basis; the product team should be broad-based; the customers' needs and wants should be known to the entire team; marketing, sales, product designers, process designers, purchasing, manufacturing, and vendors should all have representation on the product team; and the product team should live with the product from preliminary design through successful production.

Once the product team has been established, the team must assess the magnitude of its task. The breadth of options here can vary from the development of a totally new product to a minor modification of an existing product. All product assumptions, customer needs, customer wants, product restrictions, and manufacturing requirements must be initially documented. Specific product goals must be established, and these goals must be accepted and embraced by the entire product team as well as upper management.

The approach for winning manufacturing product development is as presented in Figures 7 and 8, but the priorities of product development will be product-specific. For example, consider the differences in priorities between the development of the personal computer and Boeing's development of the 767. IBM's number-one priority was to get into the marketplace quickly. The development costs were relatively low (as compared to the size of the market) and the development risks were low (Apple and Tandy had already defined the market requirements). At the same time, IBM's absence from the marketplace was beginning to cut into IBM's office market. IBM needed a product immediately.

Boeing's number-one priority was to maximize the fit of the product to the market at launch. The development costs were huge. The design requirements and market desires were not well defined. Several technological questions were unanswered. Boeing did not need a product immediately; they needed methodical, detailed, refined research and development.

Both IBM and Boeing used the winning manufacturing product development approach, but the priorities were completely different. For your winning manufacturing product development, you must determine your own priorities, then follow the integrated, iterative product development approach.

REFERENCES

Boothroyd, G., and Dewhurst, P. 1988. Product design for manufacture and assembly. *Manufacturing Engineering*. April. Vol. 100, No. 4.

Bower, J.L., and Hout, T.M. 1988. Fast-cycle capability for competitive power. *Harvard Business Review*. November-December. Vol. 66, No. 6.

Dean, J.W. Jr., and Susman, G.L. 1989. Organizing for manufacturable design. *Harvard Business Review*. January-February. Vol. 67, No. 1.

Dixon, J.R., and Duffey, M.R. 1988. Quality is not accidental: it's designed. *The New York Times*. June 26. Vol. 137, no. 47548.

Gunn, T.G. 1987. *Manufacturing for Competitive Advantage: Becoming a World Class Manufacturer*. Ballinger Publishing Company. Cambridge, Massachusetts.

Hunt, V.D. 1988. Thinking mechatronically. *Managing Automation*. February. Vol. 3, No. 2.

Krubasik, E.G. 1988. Customize your product development. *Harvard Business Review*. November-December. Vol. 66, No. 6.

Lowell, J. 1988. No threat: *Wards Auto World* finds engineers calm over outsourcing. *Wards Auto World*. March. Vol. 24, no. 3.

Martin, J.M. 1988. The final piece to the puzzle. *Manufacturing Engineering*. September. Vol. 101, No. 3.

Schonberger, R.J. 1986. *World Class Manufacturing*. Free Press. New York.

Stoll, H.W. 1988. Design for manufacture. *Manufacturing Engineering*. January. Vol. 100, No. 1.

Vasilash, G.S. 1987. Simultaneous engineering: management's new competitiveness toll. *Production*. July. Vol. 99, No. 7.

Waterman, R.H. 1987. *The Renewal Factor: How the Best Get and Keep the Competitive Edge*. Bantam Books. New York.

Winter, D. 1988. Technical outsourcing: reach out and touch someone. *Wards Auto World*. March. Vol. 24, no. 3.

Chapter 5
GLOBAL MARKETPLACE

ALL MANUFACTURING DECISIONS MUST BE MADE WITHIN THE CONTEXT OF AN INTEGRATED GLOBAL STRATEGY.

Some managers view the global marketplace as an economic, governmental, or political issue. To the contrary, the global marketplace is a winning manufacturing issue. In fact, in today's world, there is no choice but to understand the global strategy implications on all manufacturing decisions.

Since the early 1970s, the annual growth in free-world trade has been double the annual growth in the Gross National Product. Free-world trade will increase ten-fold from 1970 to the early 1990s, and will double from 1980 to the early 1990s. The huge growth in free-world trade has resulted in the involvement of most companies, to some degree, in the global marketplace. This involvement may be through:

1. Export of products,
2. Import of materials or components,
3. Foreign partners or subsidiaries, or
4. Foreign competition.

Whatever your involvement today, your future global involvement will be greater.

The increased involvement in the global marketplace is not a result of the increased interrelatedness of the world (satellite communications and efficient global travel), nor of the increased integration of political and economic systems. Of course, these issues simplify a company's involvement, but they are not what motivates a company to be involved with the global marketplace; survival is. There really is no choice.

To fully understand why you must be global, please consider the following:

1. The cost of winning manufacturing product development is greater than the cost of traditional product development.
2. Technology continues to have an increasingly important role in product development. Particularly, new materials and new electronics are affecting product development.
3. Product lives are shorter and shorter. Future shock is a reality, and product life cycles continue to decrease.
4. Because of the above three points, higher product development costs must be amortized over a shorter product life. This can be done by either:

   a. Allocating more of the product development cost to each unit sold, or
   b. Increasing the number of units sold.

Option 4a is unacceptable, because it will increase the manufacturing costs. This is contrary to the Chapter 2 Requirement of Success; significantly reducing manufacturing costs.

Option 4b would spread the higher product development cost over a larger number of units. However, with the shorter product life, the only alternative to selling more units is to expand your marketplace. This marketplace expansion directly leads to the Requirement of Success of the global marketplace.

In many industries, the global marketplace has already eliminated any company that did not think globally. For example, Japanese manufacturers pursued the global marketplace for the VHS video camcorder. Today, if you buy a VHS video camcorder, it is a Japanese product.

Thus, the three key issues that must be addressed to achieve a winning manufacturing global strategy are:

1. Global product development,
2. Global manufacturing, and
3. Global logistics.

The next three sections address these issues.

GLOBAL PRODUCT DEVELOPMENT

Some believe that the United States, Western Europe, and Japan have become a homogeneous market where identical products are desired by the marketplace, exemplified by McDonald's hamburgers, Ford's Escort, Coca-Cola's beverages, and IBM's computers. Those who believe in the homogeneous market concept believe the Chapter 4 traditional product development approach to global product development is satisfactory. Once a product for one of these markets is developed, the identical product is thrown over the wall or if you prefer, across the pond. The expectation here is that a successful world product is a product that without any customization is applicable worldwide.

Quite to the contrary, not even the straightforward examples of a McDonald's hamburger, a Ford Escort, a Coke, or an IBM computer are identical products around the world. Even the king of standardization, McDonald's, serves a different hamburger in Germany than in England. The Escort purchased in France is considerably different than the Escort purchased in California. In fact, the Escort purchased in France is different than the Escort purchased in Italy, and the Escort purchased in California is different from the Escort purchased in Michigan. Similarly, the Coca-Cola products sold in England are significantly different from the Coca-Cola products in Denmark, which are different from the Coca-Cola products in the United States. Similarly, in Europe alone, IBM has over twenty different computer keyboards.

Thus, the definition of a world product or a global product is not a product that without customization is sold around the world. The correct definition of a world product or a global product is a product that has been developed while considering the needs for global customization, and because of a standardized product platform may be manufactured by standardized, flexible manufacturing systems for consumption in the global marketplace. Thus, certainly not identical around the world, McDonald's hamburger, Ford's Escort, Coca-Cola's beverages, and IBM's computers are world products.

Chapter 3 states: "As customers become more sophisticated, they demand a higher level of product customization. The number of options available to customers will continue to increase, and winning manufacturing must have the ability to respond to this customization requirement." This trend applies not only within any given country, but even more importantly among countries. Winning global manufacturing must address the needs for domestic and international customization; winning global manufacturers must include the needs for this customization while the product is being developed. The marketing, sales, vendors, and customers referred to in the model of winning manufacturing product development (Figure 8) must include marketing sales, vendors, and customers' perspectives for the entire world.

GLOBAL MANUFACTURING

Global manufacturing can be viewed from the perspectives of off-shore global manufacturing and global networks. The following examples illustrate each of these perspectives:

Offshore Global Manufacturing

In an effort to reduce the costs of manufacturing, an electronics company had decided to have its printed circuit boards assembled and tested in Korea. The company made a common mistake and compared its fully burdened in-house standard cost of the printed circuit board to the unburdened, offshore standard cost for the printed circuit board. The annual production forecast was for one million printed circuit boards and had a fully burdened in-house standard cost of $6.54. An analysis resulted in the unburdened, offshore cost for the printed circuit board of:

F.O.B. Cost	$4.02
Overseas Buying Commission	.09
Duty	.65
User Fee	.08
Ocean Freight	.21
Insurance	.04
Broker Charge	.11
Subtotal: Landed US	$5.20
Inland Freight	.06
Total Standard Cost	$5.26

Management subtracted $6.54 from $5.26 and decided there was a $1.28 per unit savings. This savings for one million units translated into an annual savings of $1,280,000, and the decision was made to ship the printed circuit boards to Korea.

A year later, a study was done indicating that although the printed circuit boards were being purchased for $5.26, there was no real savings. In fact, an increased burden existed for the remaining products in the plant. This surprised management, who then commissioned a study of burden. The study concluded that the increase in burden was attributed to the following factors:

1. **Inventory**. Less responsiveness and longer transport times resulted in both transit and in-plant inventories increasing.
2. **Purchasing**. The physical separation, monetary fluctuations, and language difficulties resulted in increased purchasing cost.
3. **Receiving**. Transport interface problems, paperwork problems, and nonstandard packaging materials resulted in increased receiving cost.
4. **Communications**. Different time zones, distances, and language problems resulted in increased vendor communications cost.

5. **Exceptions**. The long distances involved and the difficulty with overseas transport resulted in increased costs of handling damaged, missing, and incorrectly labeled goods.
6. **Quality**. The long distances involved and the difficulty of communicating expectations and changes in expectations resulted in increased quality costs.
7. **Environment**. The managerial frustration of dealing with different cultural, legal, and political factors resulted in a loss of efficiency and thus, increased administrative costs.

An assessment of these costs resulted in a fully burdened offshore unit cost of $6.80 or $.26 per unit more than the fully burdened in-house cost per printed circuit board. Thus, although management thought they would save $1,280,000 by shipping the printed circuit boards offshore, what occurred was an increase in costs of $260,000.

The lesson to be learned from this example is that burden does not disappear when products are shipped offshore. In fact, shipping products offshore often increases burden. Therefore, the cost savings potential of shipping products offshore is oftentimes more myth than fact.

Global Networks

Winning global manufacturing is nothing more than a network of winning manufacturing operations. Figure 9 presents an example of such a network for the automotive industry.

The networks of operations evolve as demand expands. The decision to expand an existing plant or build a new plant typically depends upon transportation costs, plant investment costs, and overhead costs. As transportation costs increase, the tendency is to have more, smaller-volume plants. As plant investment and overhead costs increase, the tendency is to have fewer, higher-volume plants.

GLOBAL LOGISTICS

Global logistics are not different from domestic logistics. They are just more complex. Global logistics complexities include:

1. Time zones,
2. Languages,
3. International fund transfers and currency transactions,
4. Customs and customs agents,
5. Government agents,

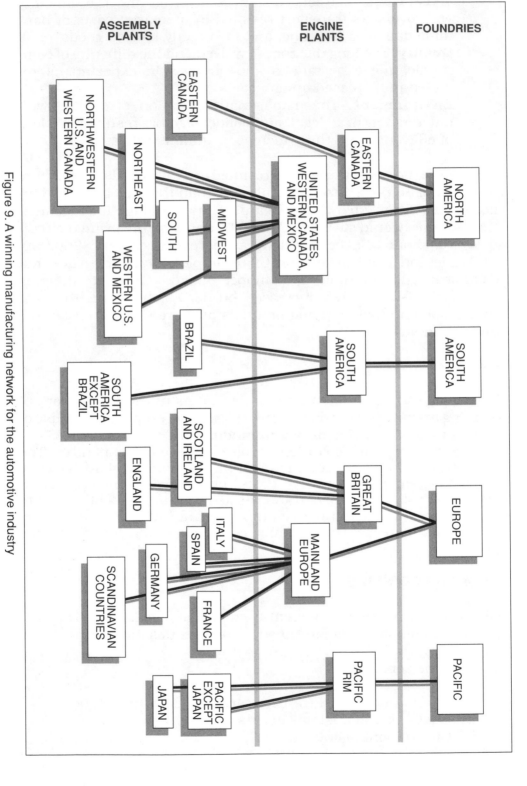

Figure 9. A winning manufacturing network for the automotive industry

6. Tariffs and trade restrictions,
7. Documentation and reporting,
8. Packaging,
9. Freight forwarders, and
10. Cultural practices.

However, just because the scope of the logistics network has been broadened and become more complex this is not a justification for allowing inefficient manufacturing to exist. Global logistics, unfortunately, have been used to justify the following inefficient manufacturing traits:

1. "We need to carry excessive inventory because global transportation times are unpredictable."
2. "Because of communications problems with our global source, we maintain a secondary source domestically."
3. "There is little value in trying to provide global suppliers with advanced information, as they never understand our needs."
4. "No loads are palletized until after they arrive in our facility, as our global suppliers don't ship in unit load quantities."
5. "You can't certify the quality of global suppliers as they are overseas."
6. "We never know what quantity of goods will be arriving until we unload the container, as the paperwork doesn't arrive until weeks after the shipment."

Obviously, these traits cannot be accepted. The only acceptable global logistics are those that support winning manufacturing. You must first understand the complexities of global logistics, and then put in place a plan for global logistics that will make the logistics network transparent to domestic or global conditions. Only then will the global marketplace become a Requirement of Success for winning manufacturing instead of an excuse for adopting losing manufacturing.

HOW TO ESTABLISH AN INTEGRATED GLOBAL STRATEGY

If your organization is active in the global marketplace, you may already be making manufacturing decisions in the context of an integrated global strategy. If so, the next step is to make certain that your global operations are moving towards winning manufacturing.

If your organization is not making decisions this way, you must develop a global strategy. The first step in establishing a global strategy is to assess your present status by answering the following questions (I have found both the federal and state Departments of Commerce helpful in providing information to answer these types of questions):

1. What global competitors do you have? What are their strengths and weaknesses? What are their present markets? How do they operate? What impact do these global competitors have on your domestic market?
2. How do your competitors' products differ from yours? What are the differences in global customers? What are the global pricing differences?
3. How well are your competitors' products standardized for global customization? How does this compare to your products? What are the trends in customization?
4. What is the global demand for your products? How will this change over the next five years? What companies have what percent of each market?
5. What constraints, restrictions, or barriers affect the free trade of your products around the globe? How will this change over the next five years?
6. What synergy could be created by increasing your participation in the global marketplace? How would this best be achieved?
7. For your company, what are the risks associated with the global marketplace? How could these risks be minimized?
8. What effect does global logistics have on your industry? On your company? What impact does logistics have on global market share?
9. What weaknesses exist in your company's global strategy? What must you do to increase your penetration of the global marketplace?
10. What global strengths does your company have? Are these strengths fully utilized? How could your company further benefit from these strengths?

Once you understand your global environment, you should establish a series of global goals. A variety of approaches to achieve these goals should be defined and evaluated. Your best global strategy should be identified, sold to management, implemented, and audited.

A group within your organization should be given the responsibility of maintaining watch on the global horizon and should actively participate in all winning manufacturing deliberations. This group should have the responsibility of being sure that all manufacturing decisions are made in the context of your integrated global strategy.

REFERENCES

Conrades, G.H. 1987. The challenge of global competition. *Vital Speeches Of The Day.* December.

Gunn, T.G. 1987. *Manufacturing for Competitive Advantage: Becoming a World Class Manufacturer.* Ballinger Publishing Company. Cambridge, Massachusetts.

Haycs, R.H., and Wheelwright, S.C. 1984. *Restoring Our Competitive Edge: Competing Through Manufacturing.* John Wiley & Sons. New York.

Kirkland, R.I. Jr. 1988. Entering a new age of boundless competition. *Fortune.* March 14. Vol. 118, no. 6.

Kupfer, A. 1988. How to be a global manager. *Fortune.* March 14. Vol. 118, no. 6.

Malone, R. 1987. Global smart factory market. *Managing Automation.* December. Vol. 2, No. 12.

Melloan, G. 1988. Global manufacturing is an intricate game. *The Wall Street Journal.* November 29.

Tompkins, J.A. 1987. Is it JIT or GM, or JIT and GM? *Industrial Product Bulletin.* May. Vol. 44, no. 5.

_____. 1987. On the one hand, but then on the other hand.... *Transportation and Distribution.* September. Vol. 28, no. 9.

_____. 1987. The myth of moving offshore. *Industrial Product Bulletin.* September. Vol. 44, no. 9.

Trunick, P.A. 1989. Global markets are changing logistics. *Transportation and Distribution.* February. Vol. 30, no. 2.

_____. 1987. *Competing in the Global Economy.* National Association of Manufacturers. Washington, D.C. April.

_____. 1989. How global is your strategy? *Production.* February. Vol. 101, No. 2.

Chapter 6
LEAD TIMES

Significant reductions in lead times must occur.

We must now move to the shop floor to create winning manufacturing operations.

Many operations set their sights on the elimination of excessive inventories. However, eliminating inventories cannot be an objective unto itself. It must result from pursuing other objectives, including reducing lead times.

WHAT IS MEANT BY LEAD TIMES?

Figure 10 illustrates the time spans that are known as manufacturing lead time, production lead time, and customer lead time. Obviously, the definitions of each differ, but people often talk about lead time reduction without really defining which of these lead times is being addressed. This is confusing.

Manufacturing lead time is that time from material availability at the first manufacturing operation until the last manufacturing operation is complete. *Production lead time* is that time from the ordering of all materials for items production, until the last manufacturing operation is complete. *Customer lead time* is that time between customer ordering and customer receipt.

UNDERSTANDING LEAD TIMES

To achieve winning manufacturing, the customer lead time must be significantly reduced. One way to do so is by reducing production lead time, and one way to reduce production lead time is by reducing manufacturing lead time.

Interestingly, studies have shown that less than 10 percent of the total manufacturing lead time in many companies is actually spent manufacturing the product. Moreover, in many companies less than

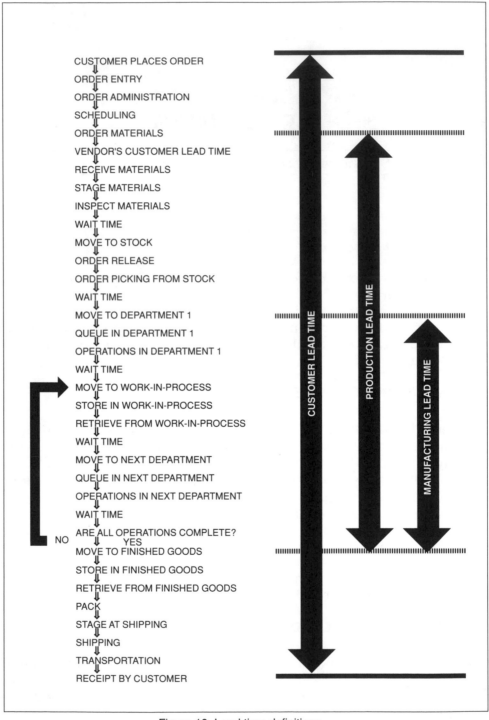

Figure 10. Lead time definitions

5 percent of the total production lead time is actually spent manu-facturing the product. And, of the total customer lead time in many companies, less than 1 percent is spent manufacturing the product.

One of my clients, for example, had a customer lead time for one of its standard products of twenty-two weeks. An analysis of my client's vendors' actual manufacturing time for all components was sixty-three minutes. The company had an additional actual manu-facturing time of eighteen minutes per unit and an assembly time of forty minutes. Thus, the total actual manufacturing time for this item with a 22-week customer lead time was 121 minutes.

Now, the obvious question is, "Why does it take twenty-two weeks to do 121 minutes of work?" When asked this question, managers responded with the following:

1. "That's just how long it takes."
2. "We are doing well; it used to take twenty-eight weeks."
3. "It has to do with the way we report production progress."
4. "I have been wondering about that myself."
5. "It must be the computer's fault."
6. "Most of the delays are due to quality problems."
7. "That's an excellent question."
8. "We have an out-of-date handling system."
9. "It doesn't really take us twenty-two weeks. We just say it does, so we are always on schedule."
10. "I don't know."

It is as if no one understands lead times. Lead times are just part of the system and trying to understand them is not anyone's job. Many believe that lead times are the result of other manufacturing decisions and are not manageable. To the contrary, lead times are as long as a company can tolerate and still stay in business. In other words, they are what management decides they should be.

The following is a typical lead time cycle:

1. A firm is consistently missing its orders by one week. Produc-tion control convinces management that if they could extend lead time one week, they could fill orders on schedule.
2. Management changes lead time from four weeks to five weeks. All customers are told of the increased lead time.
3. Because lead times are longer, the customers increase their orders. The backlog grows, and production control once again convinces management to increase lead times.
4. Management adds another week to the lead time. All custom-ers are told of the increased lead time.
5. Steps 3 and 4 are repeated until lead time grows to eighteen weeks.

6. Customers are driven away by the eighteen-week lead time. They stop ordering from the company and the backlog is reduced.
7. As management sees the backlog reduced, they believe they are gaining on the problem, and thus, they reduce lead time by one week. All customers are told of the reduced lead time.
8. Customers do not order additional products because with the reduced lead time, they already have sufficient stock ordered. Backlog is further reduced.
9. Steps 7 and 8 are repeated until lead times are drastically reduced down to original levels.
10. Things go well until a supplier has a delivery problem and some orders are missed. The process returns to Step 1 and the cycle is repeated.

Throughout the above typical lead time cycle:

1. The manufacturing system did not change,
2. The customer requirements did not change, and
3. Customer lead times varied from four weeks to eighteen weeks.

The only explanation for the tremendous variations in customer lead times is a total—but common— misunderstanding of lead times, which results in management's belief that increasing lead times gives manufacturing a better opportunity to respond to manufacturing problems.

Winning manufacturing knows that increasing lead times to improve control over the shop floor is like trying to put out a fire by dousing it with gasoline. Winning manufacturing demands shorter lead times because it knows:

1. Long lead times make it impossible to plan and control priorities,
2. Shorter lead times clear the shop floor of work-in-process inventory, conflicting manufacturing priorities, and manufacturing problems, and
3. The only controllable lead times are short lead times.

WINNING MANUFACTURING LEAD TIMES

Lead-time reductions in winning manufacturing will do more than reduce inventories. Because customers benefit from receiving their orders quickly, your market share will increase. Employees will be more satisfied because they will be working for a more responsive, more successful company. Even quality will improve. John Young, the chief executive officer of Hewlett-Packard, says, "Doing it fast forces you to do it right the first time." Of course, the effect of all these factors is the overall reduction of the costs of manufacturing.

The obtainable reduction in lead time for a company depends upon the historical approach to lead time and the amount of product customization. The less attention that has been focused on lead time, the greater the opportunity for lead time reduction. Similarly, the less customization in a product, the greater the opportunity for lead time reduction.

Table 7 illustrates the lead times for traditional and winning manufacturing for medium customization, low customization and no customization. The traditional manufacturing scenario considered in Table 7 is not a worst case but a typical manufacturing operation. The no-customization scenario presented in the table is for a standardized, no-option product line. The medium-customization scenario is for a standardized product line with many options. The high-customization, or job-shop illustration, is not included in Table 7 because the great range of lead times makes it impossible to present valid statistics.

The General Electric Plant in Salisbury, North Carolina, provides an example of reduced lead times. Circuit breaker boxes were produced with an order-to-finished-goods time of three weeks. By significantly streamlining and automating its operation, GE was able to reduce order-to-finished-goods time to three days. The benefits have been better than expected. The plant's backlog has gone from two months to two days, productivity has increased at the rate of 20 percent per year, manufacturing costs have dropped 30 percent, and return on investment is over 20 percent.

Another example is Motorola, which now produces pagers in two hours that used to take three weeks. Brunswick has reduced lead time on its fishing reels from three weeks to one week, and Hewlett-Packard has reduced lead time on its electronic testing equipment from four weeks to five days.

HOW TO SIGNIFICANTLY REDUCE LEAD TIMES

The methods of doing business must be changed in order to significantly reduce lead times. A common mistake is to try to reduce lead times by simply trying to work faster. Working faster will not result in sustained reductions in lead times.

The procedure that should be followed to reduce lead times is as follows:

1. **Document present customer lead time**. This document should be a flow chart (Figure 10), with the times recorded for each activity. The flow chart should accurately document what actually occurs, not what your standard operating

TABLE 7
Winning And Traditional Manufacturing Lead Times

LEAD TIME ACTIVITIES	LEAD TIMES (IN DAYS)						WINNING MANUFACTURING CHARACTERISTICS
	CUSTOMIZATION						
	HIGH		MEDIUM		LOW		
	Trad. Mfg.	Winning Mfg.	Trad. Mfg.	Winning Mfg.	Trad. Mfg.	Winning Mfg.	
Preproduction – Customer Order – Order Entry – Order Admin. – Scheduling – Order Materials	2	.5	2	.5	1	0	Highly computerized with low or no human involvement. Customers will enter orders via electronic data interchange. When engineering is required, it will be done through the use of computer-aided engineering.
Vendors' Customer Lead Times	20	3	10	0	5	0	Only winning manufacturing vendors will supply materials to winning manufacturing firms. In no- and low-customization environments, materials will be on-hand based upon a level production master production schedule.
Receiving – Receive Materials – Stage Materials – Inspect Materials – Wait Time – Move To Stock – Order Release – Order Picking From Stock – Wait Time – Move To Dept. 1	3	.5	3	0	3	0	All winning manufacturing materials will be preinspected. Materials will flow directly from receiving to Department 1.
Manufacturing – Queue in Dept. 1 – Operations In Dept. 1 – Wait Time – Move To Work-In-Process – Store In Work-In-Process Inventory – Retrieve From Work-In-Process Inventory – Repeat As Necessary – To Finished Goods	5	1	4	1	3	.2	By reducing production lot sizes and setup time (Chapter 7) and making material flow efficient (Chapter 15), the manufacturing lead times will be reduced significantly.
SUBTOTAL Order To Finished Goods	30	5	19	1.5	12	.2	
Postproduction – Store In Finished Goods – Retrieve From Finished Goods – Pack – Stage At Shipping – Shipping – Transportation – Receipt By Customer	5	2	5	2	5	2	Most items will be made to order, so finished goods will flow from the end of the production line out through shipping.
TOTAL Order To Receipt	35	7	24	3.5	17	2.2	

procedures manual would like you to believe occurs.

2. **Competitive analysis**. You must know your competitors' customer lead times. The more information that can be obtained about domestic and foreign competition customer lead times, the better.

3. **Leadership must establish a goal**. This goal must be more than saying, "Let's cut customer lead time from five weeks to three days." The goal must include the commitment to reduce customer lead times by doing the analysis and rethinking the methods of doing business.

4. **Identify bottlenecks**. The flow chart of the present customer lead time should be used as a beginning point. On this flow chart, the goals for each activity should be recorded. To assure meeting the overall customer lead time goal, the sum of the goals for each activity should surpass the reduction required to achieve the goal. That is, if the goal is to reduce customer lead time to three days, the sum of the goals for each of the activities should be two or two-and-a-half days. Then, when individual activity goals are not met, the overall customer lead time goal is not in jeopardy.

5. **Create multidepartment teams**. Establish teams of broad-based individuals to focus on specific sets of activities. Give the team the authority and responsibility to change the methods of business to achieve the lead-time goals. These teams should only exist for as long as is required to implement their recommendations. These teams should focus on:

   a) **Simplification**. Products, processes, organizational structures, operating systems, procedures, and methods must be simplified. (Chapter 19 presents the simplification Requirement of Success.)

   b) **Teamwork**. All internal and external organizational barriers and relationships must be eliminated. All communications must be clear, straightforward, and nonpolitical. (Chapter 18 describes the Requirement of Success of team players.)

   c) **Uncertainty**. All uncertainly must be eliminated. Everyone within your organization must understand that there is no excuse for delays. Clear schedules should be established and met. A disciplined, predictable approach must be adopted. (Chapter 8 presents the Requirement of Success of uncertainty.)

REFERENCES

Abegglen, J.C., and Stalk, G. Jr. 1985. *Kaisha: the Japanese Corporation*. Basic Books, Inc. New York.

Bower, J.L., and Hout, T.M. 1988. Fast-cycle capability for competitive power. *Harvard Business Review*. November-December. Vol. 66, No. 6.

Dumaine, B. 1989. How managers can succeed through speed. *Fortune*. February 13. Vol. 119, no. 5.

Plossl, G.W., and Welch, W.E. 1979. *The Role of Top Management in the Control of Inventory*. Reston Publishing Company, Inc. Reston, Virginia.

Schonberger, R.J. 1986. *World Class Manufacturing*. Free Press. New York.

Wight, O.W. 1974. *Production and Inventory Management in the Computer Age*. Cahners Books. Boston, Massachusetts.

_____. 1983. Reduce inventory costs with just-in-time production. *Warehouse Supervisors Bulletin*. National Foreman's Institute. July 25.

_____. 1986. What do you mean by just-in-time? *Modern Materials Handling*. August. Vol. 41, No. 9.

Chapter 7
PRODUCTION LOT SIZES

PRODUCTION LOT SIZES AND SETUP TIMES MUST BE REDUCED.

Chapter 6 stressed the importance of reducing customer lead times. This chapter focuses on the manufacturing lead-time component of customer lead times.

THE RELATIONSHIP BETWEEN MANUFACTURING LEAD TIME AND PRODUCTION LOT SIZES

The key to reducing manufacturing lead time is to reduce *dwell time*, or the length of time from item completion on one operation until the time the same item is started in the next operation. Dwell time consists of *queue time* and *material handling time*.

Material handling time is the time for material handling from one operation to the next. Material handling times here are assumed to be zero.

The impact of queue time on manufacturing lead times is illustrated in the following example:

Production Requirement = 50
Number of Operations = 3
Operation Times = 1 minute per operation

Figure 11 shows that if a production lot size of one is processed through the three operations (with conveyance time of zero and the next operation is available), the total manufacturing lead time would be fifty-two minutes.

To the contrary, Figure 12 illustrates that if a production lot size of fifty (with conveyance time of zero and the next operation is available) were pushed through these three operations, the manufacturing lead time would be 150 minutes. For this example, the increase in manufacturing lead times when the production lot size increases from a lot of one to a lot of fifty is 288 percent (52 minutes to 150 minutes).

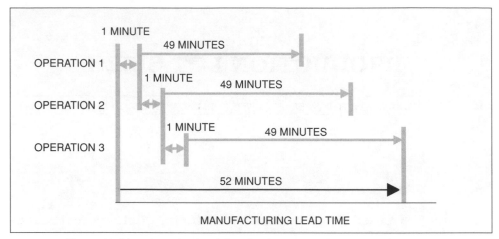

Figure 11. Manufacturing lead time for three one-minute operations, production lot size 1

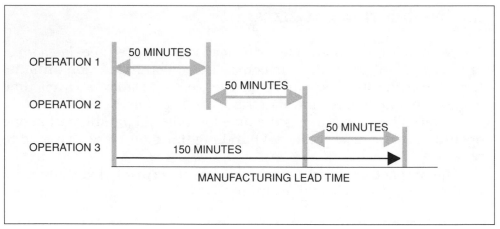

Figure 12. Manufacturing lead time for three one-minute operations, production lot size 50

Figure 13 illustrates the effect of production lot sizes on the manufacturing lead time for producing 100 units through a range of two to eight one-minute operations, assuming conveyance time is zero and the next operation is available. The figure shows that the larger the number of operations, the greater the effect the production lot size has on manufacturing lead time (see Table 8).

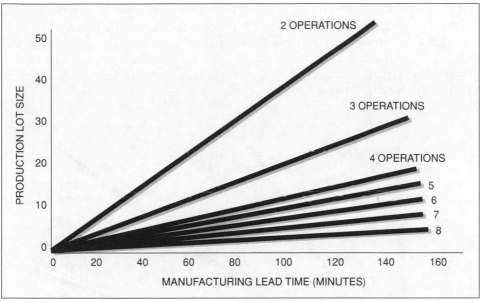

Figure 13. Impact of production lot sizes on manufacturing lead times

THE RELATIONSHIP BETWEEN PRODUCTION LOT SIZES, SETUP TIMES, AND MANUFACTURING EFFICIENCY

Figure 14 illustrates the effect of lot size and setup time on the manufacturing efficiency of a one-minute operation. For example, for a lot size of 600 and a setup time of sixty minutes, the manufacturing efficiency would be one part every 1.1 minutes (one minute of operation plus [60/600] minutes of setup time). To achieve this same

TABLE 8
The Effect Of Production Lot Size On Manufacturing Lead Times
(Processing 100 units through one-minute operations)

NUMBER OF OPERATIONS	MANUFACTURING LEAD TIME FOR LOT SIZE OF TWO (IN MINUTES)	MANUFACTURING LEAD TIME FOR LOT SIZE OF EIGHT (IN MINUTES)	PERCENT INCREASE IN MANUFACTURING LEAD TIME FOR AN INCREASE IN LOT SIZE FROM TWO TO EIGHT
2	102	108	6%
3	104	116	12%
4	106	124	17%
5	108	132	22%
6	110	140	27%
7	112	148	32%
8	114	156	37%

manufacturing efficiency while reducing the production lot size would require an equivalent reduction in the setup time.

Thus, one way to reduce inventories is to reduce customer lead times by reducing manufacturing lead times, and one way to reduce manufacturing lead times is to reduce production lot sizes by reducing setup times.

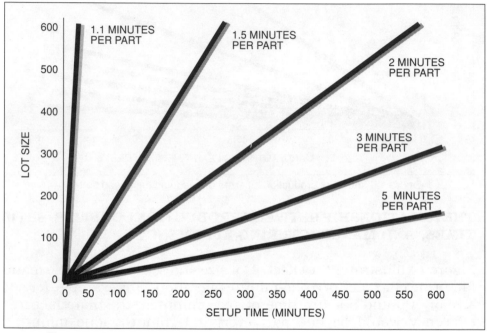

Figure 14. Impact of lot size and setup time on manufacturing efficiency

ECONOMIC LOT SIZES

The traditional approach to economic lot sizes says that the lot size that is most economical is the lot size where the setup cost equals the inventory carrying cost. This tradeoff is logical because as the production lot size becomes larger, the required number of setups is reduced, and thus, the cost of set-up is reduced and the inventory carrying costs become larger.

The traditional approach has been to continually define increasingly sophisticated mathematics to determine the optimal economic lot size. However, a look at the most basic economic lot size mathematics is sufficient.

The setup cost for a year is simply the cost per setup (S) multiplied by the number of setups per year. If the annual usage of an item is A items, and the economic lot size is Q, then the number of setups per year is A÷Q. Thus, the setup costs for a year are AS÷Q.

The inventory carrying cost for a year is the cost of carrying inventory (I) multiplied by the average value of items in inventory. The average inventory level over a year's time (assuming constant demand and replenishment to occur when inventory is depleted) is one-half of the economic lot size; that is $Q \div 2$. If the unit cost of an item in inventory is C, then the inventory carrying cost for a year is $ICQ \div 2$.

Therefore, recognizing that the economic lot size occurs when the setup costs equal the inventory carrying costs, the economic lot size occurs when:

$$\frac{AS}{Q} = \frac{ICQ}{2}$$

Cross multiplying

$$2AS = ICQ^2$$

then

$$Q^2 = \frac{2AS}{IC}$$

or the traditional economic lot size equation

$$Q = \sqrt{\frac{2AS}{IC}}$$

The difficulties with the economic lot size equation result from the following:

1. The assumptions that demand is constant and replenishment will occur when inventory is depleted,
2. The assumption that the annual usage of an item is accurately known, and
3. The assumption that the setup costs, inventory carrying costs, and unit cost of an item in inventory are known.

At best, the annual usage is a forecast, the setup costs and inventory carrying costs are estimates, and the unit cost is a guess. Thus, the economic lot size calculation is the square root of a forecast times an estimate, divided by an estimate times a guess. It is truly interesting when this level of precision results in an economic lot size with accuracy of two decimal places.

The sophistication of the economic lot size formula and the

precision of the economic lot size mathematics are not important. What is important is to understand that the traditional economic lot size methodology is a valid portion of winning manufacturing when winning manufacturing factors are used in the equation.

Winning manufacturing factors are:

A = Annual usage. This is a range of annual forecasts, typically an optimistic forecast and a pessimistic forecast. This range of forecasts will result in a range of economic lot sizes. The economic lot size selected should be the lot size within the range that best conforms to the material handling system requirements. That is, if the calculated range for Q was 7.6 to 15.3 parts per lot and twelve parts nicely fit into a standard tote pan, then the economic lot size would be twelve.

S = Cost per setup. Winning manufacturing setup costs will be low.

I = Inventory carrying costs. Traditionally, the value used as the costs of carrying inventory has been 25 percent. This is not correct. An accurate cost of carrying inventory is 35 percent to 45 percent. Inventory carrying costs include:
1. Cost of capital,
2. Space ownership cost (lease or amortization costs),
3. Space operating cost (taxes, insurance, maintenance, and energy),
4. Inventory management cost (labor, taxes and systems), and
5. Inventory shrinkage cost (damage, obsolescence, loss, or theft).

C = Unit cost. The unit cost of each part will be significantly reduced due to winning manufacturing.

The winning manufacturing economic lot sizes can be determined once these winning manufacturing factors are established.

HOW TO REDUCE SETUP TIMES

Toyota Motor Company, developed four concepts to reduce setup times and six techniques for applying these concepts. The four concepts are:

1. **Separate the internal setup from the external setup**. Internal setups are setup activities that must occur inside a machine and require that it not be in operation. External setups are setup activities that occur external to the machine and can take place while the machine is in operation. The key is to be certain that all external setup operations are completed

before the machine is taken out of production. Only internal setup activities should be performed when a machine is out of operation.

2. **Convert as much of the internal setup as possible to external setup**. Thus, by altering the machine or the setup activities, the total setup time can be minimized.

3. **Eliminate the adjustment process**. A significant percentage of all internal setups is time for adjustments. By altering the machines or the setup, a standard setting or an automatic setting can be established that eliminates the need for adjustment.

4. **Abolish the setup**. One way to eliminate setups is by standardizing parts and thus eliminating the need for a setup. Another approach is to have parallel operations performing different operations and, by a switching mechanism, use only the operations that apply to each product.

The six Toyota techniques for applying these concepts are:

1. **Standardize the external setup actions**. By standardizing the methodology for preparing dies, tools, and materials, the setup operations become less of a craftsman task and more of a routine production task.

2. **Standardize the machines**. The portions of the machines that affect setup methodology should be standardized. Standardize all functions that will result in a more routine setup operation.

3. **Use quick fasteners**. Time-consuming nut-and-bolt fastening should be replaced with quick- release, quick-fastening devices.

4. **Use a supplementary tool**. Instead of mounting a tool into a machine, it is often quicker to preset the tool into a supplementary tool and then have a quick insert of the supplementary tool into the machine.

5. **Consider multiperson setup crews**. Significant portions of the setup can be done simultaneously by different people.

6. **Automate the setup process**. The setup of some machines can be done at the touch of a button.

These techniques and concepts have been applied at Toyota to reduce what were once several-hour setups to setups of less than ten minutes, and in some circumstances, less than one minute. Thus, by reducing setup times, high-variety, high-productivity, low-inventory, small-production lot size manufacturing is a reality. This is winning manufacturing.

HOW TO REDUCE PRODUCTION LOT SIZES

Production lot sizes should be reduced as follows:

1. Document present lot sizes,
2. Identify specific lot sizes for reduction,
3. Reduce setup times by following the Toyota Motor Company technique and concepts,
4. Calculate the economic lot size,
5. Identify alternative methods for handling the economic lot size between operations,
6. Evaluate alternative methods for efficient material handling,
7. Justify the investment required to reduce setup times and to efficiently handle materials, with the savings resulting from the reduction in lot size,
8. Define and obtain support for specific improvement plans, and
9. Implement the reduced setup time and the material handling equipment as justified and begin production of reduced lot sizes.

REFERENCES

Abegglen, J.C., and Stalk, G. Jr. 1985. *Kaisha: The Japanese Corporation*. Basic Books, Inc. New York.

Monden, Y. 1983. *Toyota Production System*. Industrial Engineering and Management Press. Norcross, Georgia.

Orlichy, J. 1975. *Material Requirements Planning: The New Way of Life in Production and Inventory Management*. McGraw-Hill Book Company. New York.

Shingo, S. 1988. *Non-Stock Production: The Shingo System for Continuous Improvement*. Productivity Press. Cambridge, Massachusetts.

Wight, O.W. 1974. *Production and Inventory Management in the Computer Age*. Cahners Books. Boston, Massachusetts.

Chapter 8
UNCERTAINTY

ALL UNCERTAINTY MUST BE MINIMIZED; DISCIPLINE MUST BE INCREASED.

Mr. Murphy of Murphy's Law fame ("If something can go wrong, it will go wrong") will not be employed by a winning manufacturing firm because there the opposite of Murphy's Law will be the norm; that is, "Everything that happens will happen according to plan."

Winning manufacturing requires that all uncertainty be minimized; there simply is not enough time to deal with any unplanned or untimely events. All activities must conform to well-established, clear standards.

Minimizing uncertainty means bringing quiet, order, and stability to manufacturing so that harmony and continuity will exist in an error-free, disruption-free, crisis-free environment. The events that have caused manufacturing heartburn, such as sloppy product development schedules, quality problems, maintenance problems, unreliable employees, untimely vendor shipments, and on and on, are not a part of winning manufacturing. As the uncertainties of these events are minimized, so too is the manufacturing heartburn.

The traditional fire-fighting manufacturing manager who specializes in managing uncertainty will be replaced by a winning manufacturing manager who specializes in managing certainty. The firefighter whose career was based on making things happen in spite of the system will no longer be needed. Crisis will be viewed as failure, not as an opportunity to demonstrate one's ability to manage. Crisis will not be solved, but will be eliminated by all activities occurring according to plan.

CREATING STANDARDS

To manage certainty, a standard of performance must be established, accepted, and followed. Everyone involved must understand

and be responsive to these same standards, which must be established for:

1. Product quality,
2. Delivery schedule,
3. Delivery quantity,
4. Process performance,
5. Process duration,
6. Machine downtime,
7. Setup duration,
8. Production methodology,
9. Part tolerances,
10. Product packaging,
11. And more.

Winning manufacturing demands that the variability allowed in these standards be considerably less than with traditional manufacturing. Only when tight standards are established and achieved can certainty be managed and winning manufacturing prevail.

ESTABLISHING DISCIPLINE

Standards are expectations. Only by stating your expectations can you hope to achieve conformance. Once standards are established, the success in achieving winning manufacturing will depend upon the discipline applied to create conformance.

Discipline is the resolve to stand behind a standard and not to accept anything other than performance at or above the standard. Winning manufacturing requires discipline that is uncompromising and applied uniformly throughout a company. There can be no exceptions. All vendors, organizational elements, and production operations must have the discipline to do it right the first time.

HOW TO MINIMIZE UNCERTAINTY

Minimizing uncertainty must begin by defining the events that have caused surprises, crises, or changes in plans. You should survey a cross section of manufacturing personnel to obtain an initial list of target events. As an ongoing activity, manufacturing personnel should record events that result in surprises, crises, or changes in plans.

The procedure presented in Figure 15 should be followed for each target event. Uncertainty will be reduced by continuously pursuing the procedure for events that cause surprises, crises, or changes in plans.

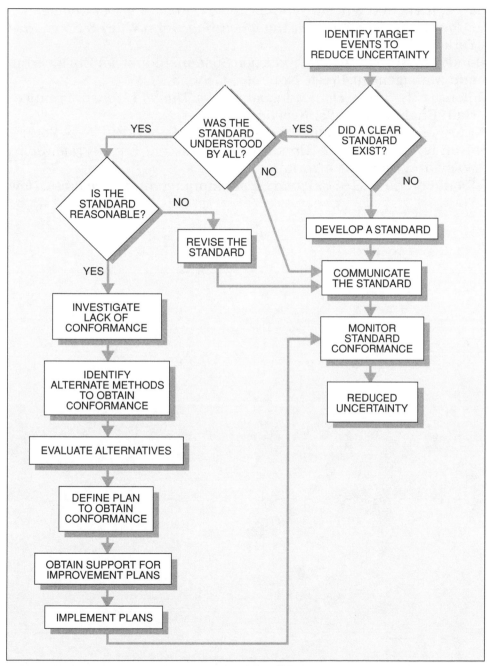

Figure 15. Reducing uncertainty

REFERENCES

Crosby, P.B. 1984. *Quality Without Tears: The Art of Hassle-Free Management.* McGraw-Hill Book Company. New York.

Hayes, R.H., and Wheelwright, S.C. 1984. *Restoring Our Competitive Edge: Competing Through Manufacturing.* John Wiley & Sons. New York.

Monden, Y. 1983. *Toyota Production System.* Industrial Engineering and Management Press. Norcross, Georgia.

Odione, G.S. 1961. *How Managers Make Things Happen.* Prentice-Hall. Englewood Cliffs, New Jersey.

Porter, M.E. 1985. *Competitive Advantage.* Free Press. New York.

Salvendy, G. Ed. 1982. *Handbook of Industrial Engineering.* John Wiley and Sons. New York.

Schonberger, R.J. 1986. *World Class Manufacturing.* Free Press. New York.

Chapter 9
BALANCE

The concept of balance is not a part of traditional manufacturing because in traditional manufacturing, the objective is to maximize machine output. In order to achieve this, several large production lots sit in work-in-process (WIP) inventory awaiting machine availability. More important than the balance of a series of operations is the speed of each individual operation.

However, in winning manufacturing, where production lot sizes and setup times are reduced and where uncertainties are minimized, there is no need for large WIP inventories. In winning manufacturing, more important than the speed of any operation will be the balance of a series of operations.

UNDERSTANDING BALANCE

The starting point in achieving balance is determining the cycle time that must be met to satisfy production requirements. For example, if your production requirement is 3,000 units per week and you have only 2,400 minutes of operation time in a week, then your cycle time is:

$$\frac{2{,}400 \text{ minutes/week}}{3{,}000 \text{ units/week}} = 0.8 \text{ minutes/unit}$$

You must produce one unit at each operation every 0.8 minutes. If you have a series of operations producing one unit every 0.8 minutes, having one of these operations producing one unit every 0.6 minutes does not increase output. It is not the speed of any one operation that is critical but rather the balance of all operations that will affect the success of the series of operations.

Achieving balance requires you to address focused departments, continuous flow, sequential flow, and standardization.

Focused Departments

Balanced operations require focused departments, which means that all the operations required to produce a family of parts are located in a focused area.

The original concept of focused departments evolved from the concept of group technology (GT) in the 1930s. The basic approach to GT was to achieve balance and production efficiency by using a team of people and a group of operations (a focused department) to produce a family of geometrically similar parts. The group of operations was integrated by a material handling system and placed into an integrated layout for the production of the specific family of parts.

In the 1960s, the concept of flexible manufacturing systems (FMS) was created as an approach to achieve the same objective as GT. The basic approach was to integrate the manufacturing equipment and the computer control into a system that was capable of producing a family of parts. Although they are often computer controlled, the essence of FMS was the same as the essence of GT. Therefore, the new approach of FMS was not really new, but rather an update of the original focused department concept of GT.

Then, in the 1980s, the concept of cellular manufacturing (CM) evolved. The objective of CM was to achieve balance and production efficiency by integrating production equipment, material handling equipment, and computer control into a focused department to produce a family of parts. The focused departments were called cells, thus the term cellular manufacturing. In reality, CM is no more than a 1980s version of GT and FMS.

Regardless of which term is preferred—GT, FMS, or CM— the key aspect in all three is to create balance. This balance comes from:

1. Focusing the operations required to produce a family of parts into a designated area, and
2. Focusing the management of the department on the combined output of all the operations.

An extension of the focused department is the concept of focused factories, which provide for the balance and support of a series of focused departments. A focused factory provides all resources required to produce the total product. Focused factories consist of focused receiving, focused departments, shipping, material handling, and management.

Focused receiving and shipping often are best accommodated by distributed receiving and shipping. (Distributed receiving and

shipping are the opposite of centralized receiving and shipping.)
With distributed receiving, material enters your facility as close as
possible to the point of use; internal material handling is minimized.
With distributed shipping, finished goods leave your facility adjacent
to the final packaging process.

Focused material handling should be viewed in layers. Within a
focused department, focused material handling equipment will move
unfinished parts between operations. Within a focused factory,
focused material handling systems will move finished parts between
focused departments. At the highest level within a manufacturing
facility, the material handling systems will be moving major sub-
assemblies between focused factories. Focused material handling
equipment and systems will be dedicated to handling specified loads
over defined flow paths.

In the automotive assembly plant given in Figure 16, the material
handling system moving automobiles between factories is a pallet
conveyor system. Within the cockpit focused factory (Figure 17), the
material handling system is an electrified monorail, which moves the
cockpit from the cockpit kitting focused department to the instrument panel subassembly focused department to the steering col-
umn-dash panel decking station and then to the mainline. At the
lowest level, the material handling system within the instrument
panel subassembly focused department (Figure 18) is a flat-top chain
conveyor.

A focused factories management system consists of all planning,
control, and reporting requirements for the focused factory. The
focused management system must consist of:

1. Production planning,
2. Material requisitioning,
3. Purchasing,
4. Receiving,
5. Material tracking,
6. Production and inventory control,
7. Financial reporting,
8. Quality assurance,
9. Order tracking,
10. Shipping,
11. And more.

The management system for each focused factory must provide
for the operation and management of the factory as an independent
operation. Winning manufacturing balance can be achieved only by
providing this level of control at the focused factory level.

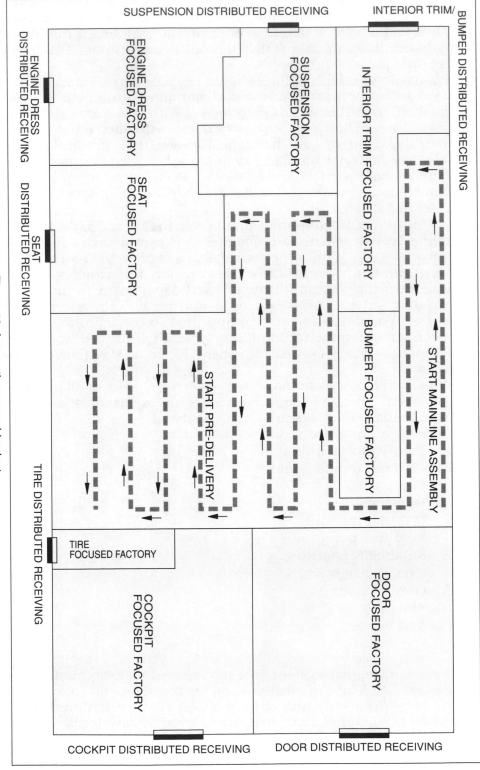

Figure 16. Automotive assembly plant

74

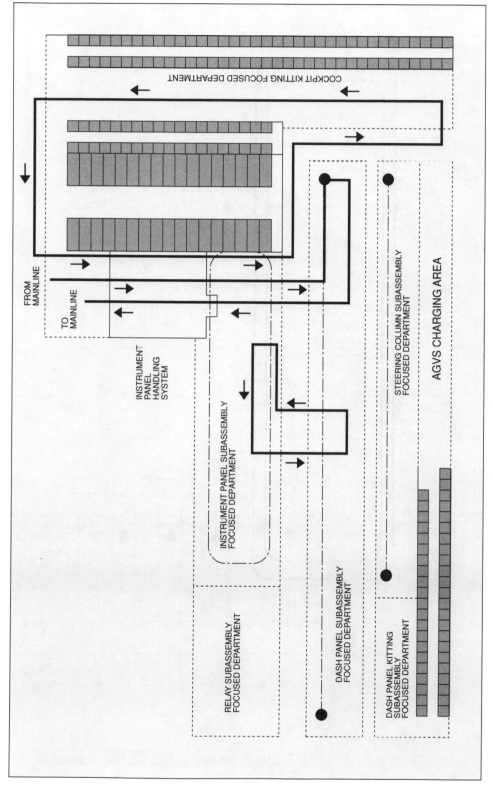

Figure 17. Cockpit focused factory

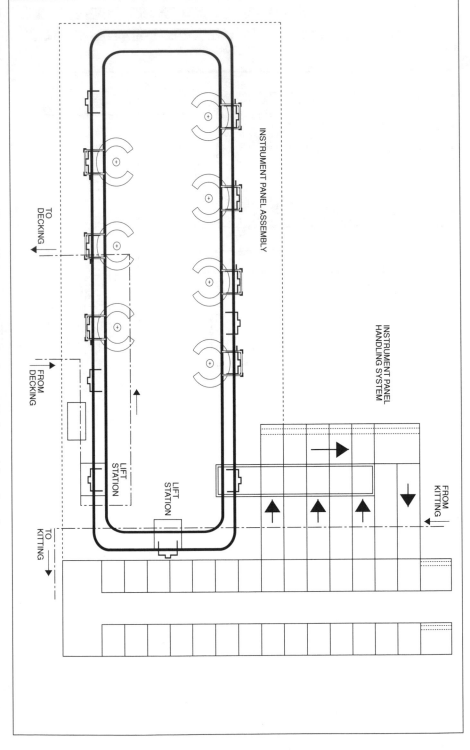

Figure 18. Instrument panel subassembly focused department

76

Continuous Flow

The production lot size Requirement of Success demands that production lot sizes be reduced. Balancing a series of operations for these reduced production lot sizes requires a continuous, controlled indexing of parts through production.

When circumstances make continuous flow impossible, the only course of action is to install WIP inventory buffers. Although undesirable, WIP inventory buffers are sometimes required. For example, if a part has a cycle time of 0.8 minutes, it is unrealistic to receive the raw material for this item every 0.8 minutes. It would be more realistic for a batch to be received, held in a WIP inventory buffer and then have one part released on a continuous basis once every 0.8 minutes.

An important distinction is the difference between a WIP inventory buffer and a traditional raw material warehouse. A WIP inventory buffer is a high-turnover, low-inventory buffer where material continuously flows. A traditional raw material warehouse is a low-turnover, high-inventory stockpile of raw materials.

Likewise, a WIP inventory buffer should be used to accommodate operations that function on different operating schedules. For example, if one focused department functions on a two-shift basis and another focused department on a one-shift basis, a WIP inventory buffer is needed between these departments to balance the shifts' production.

Another important distinction is the difference between a WIP inventory buffer and a traditional WIP storeroom. A WIP inventory buffer is a high-turnover, low-inventory buffer where material continuously flows. A traditional WIP storeroom is a low-turnover, high-inventory stockpile of WIP materials.

As a general rule, balance can best be achieved by the continuous flow of parts through production. When this rule cannot be met due to receiving or scheduling requirements, WIP inventory buffers should be installed. These buffers are not long-term storage locations, but instead, mere hesitations in the continuous flow of material.

Sequential Flow

True continuous-flow balance can only occur when the sequence of parts flowing through a series of operations is unchanged. If the first operation produces the sequence of production lots A-B-C-D and the second operation must produce in the sequence B-D-A-C, continuous flow is not possible. To accommodate the change in production lot sequences, a WIP inventory buffer is required for resequencing.

Teamwork and an integration with your vendors are required in order to receive parts in the proper sequence (see Chapters 18 and

20). When vendors cannot be given the proper sequencing information, a WIP inventory buffer is required for resequencing.

As in the case where continuous flow could not be maintained and WIP inventory buffers were installed, when sequential flow cannot be maintained, WIP inventory buffers should be installed as high-turnover, low-inventory, hesitations in the continuous flow of materials.

Standardization

To achieve balance, all operations must be performed with certainty. Uncertainty destroys balance. The achievement of certainty requires that a standard of performance be established, accepted, and followed.

Likewise, the achievement of balance requires that a standard of performance be established, accepted, and followed for each operation, focused department, and focused factory.

At Toyota Motor Company, the procedure for establishing standard operations is as follows:

1. **Determine the cycle time**. As previously defined, the cycle time is the time available to produce one unit at each operation.
2. **Determine elemental time**. The elemental time is the time required to perform the work elements. Elemental times consist of operator time and machine time.
3. **Determine the standard operations routine**. The standard operations routine is the assignment of work elements to operations. The allocation of work elements to operations must be done so that each operation can finish all the assigned work elements within the specified cycle time.
4. **Determine the standard quantity of WIP**. The standard quantity of WIP is the quantity of material within the focused factory. The production lot size and the number of lots between production operations will dictate the standard quantity of WIP. When setup times are reduced, so too are the production lot sizes. The best approach to determine the standard quantity of WIP is to simulate the focused factory while considering a variety of production schedules. The results of the simulation will be the actual focused factory performance and the quantity of WIP to support this performance.
5. **Document the standard of performance**. This standard of performance should specify:
   a) what consistent performance will result from your opera-

tions, focused departments and focused factories; and
b) how the operations, focused departments, and focused factories should be operated to achieve the specified performance.

Once established, the standard operations must then be accepted and followed. It is only by pursuing the standard operations that all operations can be performed with certainty and thus, balance be achieved.

MANAGING BALANCE

We now have to face reality: no manufacturing operation will ever achieve total balance. In fact, the objective of balance must be placed in the context of the Requirement of Success of reducing the costs of manufacturing. If you understand the implications of manufacturing costs, then balance can be properly managed.

For example, a manufacturing company, where the cost to process a receipt is $30, has a demand for one pallet of components per day. Considering twenty-two working days per month, the monthly demand is twenty-two pallets. The cost of carrying a pallet of components a month is $50. The transportation costs for the delivery of pallets is given in Table 9. The question is, how much material should be delivered at what frequency?

A theoretical balance perspective suggests that one pallet be delivered each day during the month (just-in-time). Certainly, this strategy comes closest to continuous flow and would minimize WIP inventory. However, from a cost perspective, a strategy of receiving one pallet per day for a month would result in a monthly cost of:

Total
Monthly = Receipt + Carrying + Transportation
Cost   Cost   Cost   Cost

Total
Monthly = (22 receipts) ($30/receipt) + (.5 average pallets in
Cost   inventory) ($50/month/pallet) + (22 deliveries) ($100/
            delivery)

Total
Monthly = $660 + $25 + $2,200
Cost

Total
Monthly = $2,885
Cost

Similarly, the monthly cost of receiving three pallets every third day would be:

Total
Monthly = (22÷3 receipts/month) ($30/receipt) + (1.5 average
Cost   pallets in inventory) ($50/month/pallet) + (22÷3 de-
liveries/month) ($120/delivery) = $220 + $75 + $880
= $1,175

TABLE 9
Transportation Costs Per Pallet

NUMBER OF PALLETS	TRANSPORTATION COSTS (IN DOLLARS)
1	$100
2	110
3	120
4	125
5	130
6	132
7	135
8	137
9	140
10	142
11	145
12	147
13	150
14	152
15	155
16	157
17	160
18	160

Table 10 presents the total monthly costs for a variety of delivery strategies. The minimal cost strategy is to receive twelve pallets of components every twelve days. Thus, although we want to receive components at a rate that will balance production, the economics of this example dictate that receiving loads once every twelve days is just-in-time.

As the costs of the components increase, different economics appear. For example, using the same demand, receipt cost, and transportation cost as the first example, Table 11 illustrates what happens when the component cost increases. The minimal cost strategy when the monthly carrying cost increases to $400 is to receive four pallets of components every four days.

Similarly, when the demand increases, different economics appear. For example, using the same receipt cost, transportation cost, and inventory carrying cost as the first example, Table 12 illustrates what happens when the component demand increases. The minimal cost

TABLE 10
Costs Of Operation For Demand Of 22 Pallets/Month And Inventory Carrying
Costs Of $50/Month/Pallet

NUMBER OF PALLETS ORDERED	MONTHLY COSTS (IN DOLLARS)			
	RECEIPT COSTS	CARRYING COSTS	TRANSPORTATION COSTS	TOTAL COSTS
1	$660.00	$25.00	$2,200.00	$2,885.00
2	330.00	50.00	1.210.00	1,590.00
3	220.00	75.00	880.00	1,175.00
4	165.00	100.00	687.00	952.00
5	132.00	125.00	572.00	829.00
6	110.00	150.00	484.00	744.00
7	94.29	175.00	424.29	693.58
8	82.50	200.00	376.75	659.25
9	73.33	225.00	342.22	640.55
10	66.00	250.00	312.40	628.40
11	60.00	275.00	290.00	625.00
12	55.00	300.00	269.50	624.50
13	50.77	325.00	253.85	629.62
14	47.14	350.00	238.86	636.00
15	44.00	375.00	227.33	646.33

strategy when the monthly demand doubles to two pallets/day (forty-four pallets/month) is to receive sixteen pallets of components every eight days.

The results of the examples are generalized as follows (see Figure 19):

1. As the cost of a component increases, the most-economical order cycle gets shorter.
2. As the demand of a component increases, the most-economical order cycle gets shorter.

TABLE 11
Monthly Costs Of Operation For Demand Of 22 Pallets/Month And Inventory
Carrying Costs Of $400/Month/Pallet

NUMBER OF PALLETS ORDERED	MONTHLY COSTS (IN DOLLARS)			
	RECEIPT COSTS	CARRYING COSTS	TRANSPORTATION COSTS	TOTAL COSTS
1	$660.00	$200.00	$2,200.00	$3,060.00
2	330.00	400.00	1,210.00	1,940.00
3	220.00	600.00	880.00	1,700.00
4	165.00	800.00	687.00	1,652.00
5	132.00	1,000.00	572.00	1,704.00
6	110.00	1,200.00	484.00	1,794.00
7	94.29	1,400.00	424.29	1,918.58

TABLE 12
Monthly Costs Of Operations For Demand Of 44 Pallets/Month And
Inventory Carrying Costs Of $50/Month/Pallet

NUMBER OF PALLETS ORDERED	MONTHLY COSTS (IN DOLLARS)			
	RECEIPT COSTS	CARRYING COSTS	TRANSPORTATION COSTS	TOTAL COSTS
1	$1,320.00	$25.00	$4,400.00	5,745.00
2	660.00	50.00	2,420.00	3,130.00
3	440.00	75.00	1,760.00	2,275.00
4	330.00	100.00	1,375.00	1,805.00
5	264.00	125.00	1,144.00	1,533.00
6	220.00	150.00	968.00	1,338.00
7	188.57	175.00	848.57	1,212.14
8	165.00	200.00	753.50	1,118.50
9	146.67	225.00	684.44	1,056.11
10	132.00	250.00	624.80	1,006.80
11	120.00	275.00	580.00	975.00
12	110.00	300.00	539.00	949.00
13	101.54	325.00	507.69	934.23
14	94.29	350.00	477.71	922.00
15	88.00	375.00	454.67	917.67
16	82.50	400.00	431.75	914.25
17	77.65	425.00	414.12	916.77
18	73.33	450.00	396.00	919.33

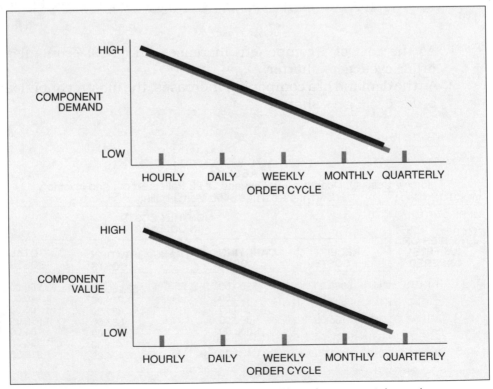

Figure 19. The relationship between order cycle and component demand
and order cycle and component value

For a high-demand, high-cost component, the order strategy may be to literally balance the rate of receiving with the rate of production; that is, just-in-time. However, for a low-demand, low-cost component, the order strategy may be to place an order once a year, place the item in storage, and floor stock a month's demand; that is, just-in-time for this component. Thus, as the production demand and the cost of a component vary, so too does the proper order strategy and the definition of just-in-time.

Available capacity is another practical issue that affects balance. If one of your operations is a capacity bottleneck, even though the best balance may not result, it may be best to build a WIP inventory buffer in front of the bottleneck to ensure full utilization of the capacity-limited operation. The size of the inventory buffer depends upon:

1. The cost of the bottleneck equipment,
2. The cost of the WIP inventory, and
3. The severity of the capacity bottleneck.

The approach to the bottleneck capacity should be:

1. To use simulation to establish the proper level of WIP inventory buffer in front of the bottleneck operation,
2. To evaluate the cost of the WIP inventory buffer versus the cost of obtaining more capacity and thus eliminating the bottleneck. (If the bottleneck is eliminated by the addition of more capacity, work towards achieving balance), and
3. If the bottleneck is not eliminated:
   a) Maximize the speed of the bottleneck operation, and
   b) Balance non-bottleneck operations to maintain the proper WIP inventory buffer in front of the bottleneck operation.

HOW TO ACHIEVE BALANCED MANUFACTURING

Because WIP inventory is a symptom of unbalanced operations, the first step in achieving balanced manufacturing is to document your present WIP inventory. Once the levels of WIP inventory have been documented, the following series of questions need to be addressed:

1. Have setup time reductions been implemented? What is the potential for setup time reductions?
2. Have production lot sizes been reduced? What is the potential for production lot size reductions?
3. Has uncertainty been minimized? What potential exists for minimization of uncertainty?

4. Have focused departments and focused factories been implemented? What opportunities exist for the creation of focused departments and focused factories?

5. Do production lots continuously flow through manufacturing operations? Are all WIP inventory buffers justifiable? Are WIP inventory buffers high-turnover, low-inventory hesitations in the continuous flow of materials?

6. Have the proper procedures been put in place to maximize sequential flow? How can WIP inventory be reduced by implementing sequential flow?

7. Have standards of performance been established, accepted and followed for each operation, focused department, and focused factory? How can the standards of performance be more rigorously pursued?

8. Have the operational costs of just-in-time been analyzed? Is there a proper understanding of the tradeoff between operating costs and balance?

9. Have capacity bottlenecks been properly analyzed? Has the issue of balance been properly addressed both before and after the capacity bottleneck?

10. If not already answered, why does WIP inventory exist? Are all WIP inventories justifiable?

The answers to these ten sets of questions will result in a listing of opportunities for achieving balanced manufacturing. These opportunities should be prioritized; alternatives identified and evaluated; and improvement plans defined, approved and implemented. Although total balance will never be realized, the winning manufacturing process of continuous improvement should lead to greater and greater balance.

REFERENCES

Monden, Y. 1983. *Toyota Production System*. Industrial Engineering and Management Press. Norcross, Georgia.

Srihanth, M.L., and Cavallaro, H.E. Jr. 1987. *Regaining Competitiveness: Putting the Goal to Work*. Spectrum Publishing Company. New Haven, Connecticut.

Tompkins, J.A. 1985. This column may not be in time. *Industrial Product Bulletin*. May. Vol. 42, no. 5.

_____. 1987. Focused factories. *Industrial Product Bulletin*. November. Vol. 44, no. 11.

White, J.A. Ed. 1987. *Production Handbook*. John Wiley & Sons. New York.

Chapter 10
PRODUCTION AND INVENTORY CONTROL

THE PRODUCTION AND INVENTORY CONTROL SYSTEM MUST BE STRAIGHTFORWARD AND TRANSPARENT.

Production and inventory control has been more frustrating and disappointing to management than any other area of manufacturing. Millions of dollars have been spent on production and inventory control systems that have not worked.

The proper direction for production and inventory control is confusing, and terminology fuels the confusion. Much is written about push systems, pull systems, kanban, just-in-time, zero inventories, stockless production, Toyota production and inventory control system, material requirements planning, and manufacturing resource planning (MRP II). Unfortunately, the meanings of these terms vary from company to company and from person to person.

The production and inventory control difficulties are an outgrowth of traditional manufacturing. In fact, the complexities of traditional manufacturing have made the effective implementation of production and inventory control systems very difficult. The keys to a winning manufacturing production and inventory control system are:

1. A production and inventory control system that is a part of the winning manufacturing process,
2. A production and inventory control system that is straightforward and transparent, and
3. A production and inventory control system that is MRP II-based.

PRODUCTION AND INVENTORY CONTROL AND WINNING MANUFACTURING

Production and inventory control in a winning manufacturing company will be radically different than production and inventory control in a traditional company. This difference will not be in the methods, but in the approach to:

1. **Manufacturing and marketing**. Because manufacturing and marketing will be working as a team, the production plan will be more predictable. Because of this predictability, production fluctuations from period to period will be minimized and product families will be produced at what will approximate a uniform rate. This more predictable production plan and more-uniform production rate will result in hassle-free, and therefore simplified, production and inventory control systems.

2. **Product development**. Because product development will become an integrated, iterative process, the number of standard components will increase, the total number of components will decrease, and the ease of changing models will increase. More simply, winning manufacturers will develop products that are easier to produce, thereby reducing the complexity of production and inventory control systems.

3. **Lead times and production lot sizes**. Because of the reduction in lead times and in production lot sizes, continuous-flow manufacturing through focused factories will be the norm. Due to the short lead times, changes in the master production schedule will be minimized. Due to the short lead times and small production lot sizes, shop floor control systems will be simplified as less material will be on the floor at one time. Reducing changes in the master production schedule and simplifying the shop-floor control system will both contribute to a simplified production and inventory control system.

4. **Uncertainty and balance**. The reduction of uncertainty and the increase in balance will result in production schedules being met. Expediting and rescheduling will be minimized and thus, even a greater likelihood will exist that schedules will be met. Consistently meeting schedules will simplify the production and inventory control system.

STRAIGHTFORWARD AND TRANSPARENT PRODUCTION AND INVENTORY CONTROL

Straightforward production and inventory control systems are systems that are easily understood; transparent ones are logical and follow intuition. Both must be based on common sense.

The objective of a production and inventory control system is to control production and inventory, and the following steps must be undertaken in order to do so:

1. Define the products, families and options to be produced,
2. Define the volume of products, families and options to be produced,
3. Specify a production plan,
4. Define when materials and capacity should be present to meet the production plan,
5. Schedule material delivery from vendors,
6. Schedule focused factories, and
7. Monitor schedule adherence.

In winning manufacturing, each step must be undertaken in a straightforward and transparent manner.

MANUFACTURING RESOURCE PLANNING

All winning manufacturing firms will have a manufacturing resource planning (MRP II) production and inventory control system. MRP II is straightforward and transparent; MRP II is no more than common sense.

The past failures of MRP II were not because the tool MRP II is wrong. The problem has been in how the tool was applied.

Figure 20 illustrates the functioning of MRP II. The first step in the MRP II process is to extract from a company's business plan the products, families, and options to be produced. The second step is to establish a production plan, based upon the business plan, that specifies the volumes of products, families, and options.

The third MRP II step is to develop the master production schedule—a detailed schedule of what specific items will be produced on what dates. The master production schedule feeds the capacity requirements planning function, where the decision is made on when certain levels of capacity must be available. The master production schedule also feeds the material requirements planning function along with input from the capacity requirement planning function. The material requirements planning function defines what materials are needed in what timeframe to meet the master production schedule.

The results of the materials requirements planning function are vendor and focused department schedules; adherence to these schedules results in production and inventory control.

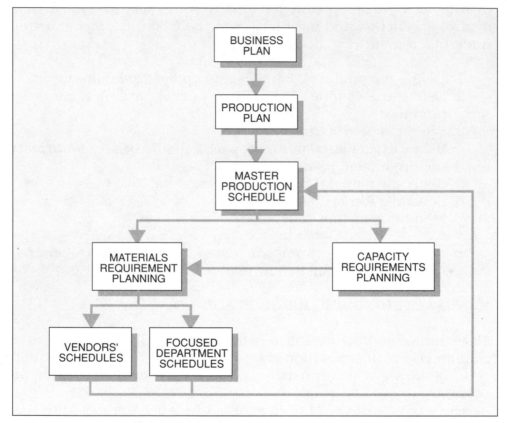

Figure 20. Manufacturing resource planning

THE TOYOTA PRODUCTION AND INVENTORY CONTROL METHODOLOGY

Figure 21 illustrates the Toyota production and inventory control methodology. The business plan and production plan functions are the same as with MRP II. Where MRP II establishes a master production schedule, the Toyota methodology establishes a uniform plant load—the rate at which products must be produced to meet the production plan. This rate is fed into a capacity requirements planning function where, just as with MRP II, the decision is made on what levels of capacity must be available. The uniform plant load

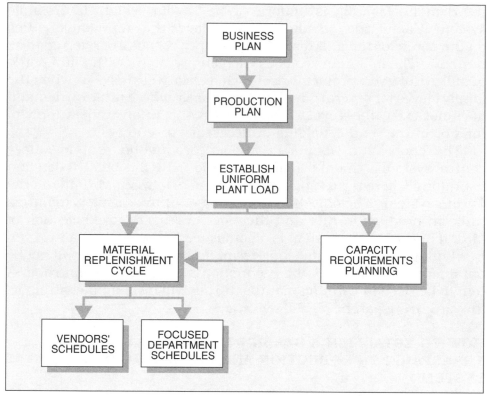

Figure 21. Toyota production and inventory control methodology

also feeds the material replenishment cycle along with input from the capacity requirements planning function. The material replenishment cycle defines what materials are needed on a regular cycle to meet the uniform plant load.

The results of the material replenishment cycle function are vendor and focused department schedules, which specify the uniform rate for material replenishment. The adherence to these rates results in production and inventory control.

The differences between MRP II and the Toyota production and inventory control may be illustrated by considering a milkman example. With MRP II, each Friday the milkman arrives and is presented with a vendor order. The vendor order is established by the homemaker comparing the quantity of milk on hand with the master production schedule for milk. If relatives with several milk drinkers are to arrive on the weekend, the master production schedule for milk will be higher, and thus, more milk will be ordered. If the family is to be away for several days, the master production schedule would indicate no milk is needed, and thus, none would be ordered.

With the Toyota production and inventory control methodology, the demand for milk is uniform. The Toyota system is a simple system. Each Friday, the homemaker places the empty milk bottles on the porch for the milkman. These empty bottles are referred to as Kanban. The milkman replaces each empty bottle with a full bottle of milk. However, problems occur when relatives arrive or when the family leaves for several days. In these cases, where uniform demand does not exist, the Toyota system will result in an undersupply of milk or in the vendor holding unnecessary inventory.

The conclusion about the proper production and inventory control system is that if demand is erratic, MRP II is best. If demand is uniform, there is no functional difference between MRP II and the Toyota system. The objective of winning manufacturing is to have a uniform production rate and therefore, in theory, the selection of MRP II or the Toyota system is a nonissue. However, in reality, even in winning manufacturing, long-term, uniform schedules will not be obtained, and therefore, the production and inventory control system to be used in winning manufacturing will be a simple, straightforward, transparent MRP II system.

HOW TO ESTABLISH A STRAIGHTFORWARD AND TRANSPARENT PRODUCTION AND INVENTORY CONTROL SYSTEM

Traditional manufacturing companies will fit within one of the following categories:

Category I: Successful MRP II User
Category II: Unsuccessful MRP II User
Category III: Nonuser of MRP II

The approach that Category I traditional manufacturing companies should take to achieve a straightforward and transparent production and inventory control system is different from the approach that should be pursued by Category II and III companies.

Successful MRP II users (Category I) must be prepared for a significant simplification of their MRP II system. As winning manufacturing is pursued, the following changes in the MRP II system will be required:

1. The MRP II "time buckets" will be made much shorter.
2. Work will not be scheduled to individual machines but to focused departments. The focused departments will be treated like a single machine.
3. Capacity requirements planning will be simplified and will only

impact production operations when changes occur in the production plan.

4. Significantly improved material tracking and control systems will provide real-time information of shop floor status. The use of this information along with the balance of focused departments will minimize work-in-process inventories and maximize the uniformity of the continuous flow of materials through production. This consistency will result in more uniform vendor and focused department schedules, which will lead to schedule conformance. The net effect of improved tracking, balance, uniformity and conformance will be a hassle-free, operating environment for MRP II. Complex MRP II operations will be replaced by streamlined, simple, straightforward, transparent MRP II operations.

Category II, unsuccessful MRP II users, should discard their MRP II systems. Category III, nonusers of MRP II, should not pursue MRP II until significant progress has been made towards winning manufacturing. The focus for both Category II and III users should be on achieving:

1. Manufacturing and marketing synergy,
2. Simplified product design,
3. Reduced lead times,
4. Reduced production lot sizes,
5. Reduced uncertainty,
6. Balanced focused departments and focused factories,
7. Reduced inventories,
8. Continuous-flow manufacturing, and
9. Improved material tracking and control.

Then, a simplified MRP II system, as described for Category I users, should be pursued.

REFERENCES

Edwards, J.N., and Anderson, J.W. 1983. Integrating JIT with MRP. *APICS Conference Proceedings*. October.

_____. 1984. Integrating JIT with MRP: an update. *APICS Conference Proceedings*. October.

Garwood, D. 1984. Explaining JIT, MRP II and Kanban. *P & IM Review*. October. Vol. 4, No. 10.

Goddard, W.E. 1986. *Just-In-Time: Surviving by Breaking Tradition.*

Cahners Books. Boston, Massachusetts.

Hall, R.W. 1983. *Zero Inventories*. Dow Jones-Irwin. Homewood, Illinois.

Monden, Y. 1983. *Toyota Production System*. Industrial Engineering and Management Press. Norcross, Georgia.

Orlichy, J. 1975. *Material Requirements Planning: The New Way of Life in Production and Inventory Management*. McGraw-Hill. New York.

Chapter 11
INVENTORIES

DRASTIC REDUCTIONS IN INVENTORIES MUST OCCUR.

Some companies have adopted the philosophy that inventories are evil. These companies often identify inventory reduction as a primary objective. It is true that inventory is expensive because of the cost of carrying inventory and manufacturing problems that are not addressed because the problems are obscured by inventory. However, just because inventory is expensive, it is not necessarily evil and you should not automatically assume that in all circumstances, all inventories should be eliminated.

Traditional manufacturing companies create inventory for what appears to be justifiable reasons. For example:

1. Finished goods inventories are created to improve customer services.
2. Work-in-process inventories are created to increase manufacturing efficiency.
3. Raw material inventories are created to take advantage of quantity discounts on raw materials.

Certainly, the objectives of improved customer service, increased manufacturing efficiency, and reduced raw material prices are admirable. Unfortunately, to be successful in pursuing these objectives, traditional manufacturing companies build large inventories.

The attempt by traditional manufacturing companies to reduce inventories can either contribute to winning manufacturing or result in failure. Eliminating the problems that lead to the creation of the inventory in a traditional manufacturing company will lead to winning manufacturing. For example:

1. Finished goods inventories may be reduced and customer service improved by significantly reducing lead times.
2. Work-in-process inventories may be reduced and manufacturing efficiency increased by significantly reducing setup times.
3. Raw material inventories may be reduced and quantity discounts still achieved by working with vendors as team players.

The attack by traditional manufacturing companies on inventories can fail if inventory reduction is viewed as an end unto itself. Eliminating inventories without resolving the problems that lead to the creation of the inventory will not lead to winning manufacturing. For example:

1. Cutting finished goods inventory while maintaining traditional manufacturing methods will result in the deterioration of customer service.
2. Cutting work-in-process inventories while maintaining traditional manufacturing methods will result in a loss of manufacturing efficiency.
3. Reducing raw materials by purchasing smaller quantities and not altering the traditional manufacturing relationship with the vendor will increase both the purchase price and the receiving cost.

The objective of winning manufacturing is to eliminate the problems that lead to the creation of the inventory. Once this objective is met the total costs of manufacturing can be reduced by drastically reducing inventories.

ATTACKING THE PROBLEMS THAT LEAD TO THE CREATION OF INVENTORY WITH WINNING MANUFACTURING

Eliminating the problems that lead to the creation of inventory can be attacked by applying the following Requirements of Success:

1. **Manufacturing and Marketing**. Manufacturing and marketing will have improved communications on customization, customer expectations, and forecasts. These improved communications will result in manufacturing better understanding its mission. The clearer the understanding of this mission, the less inventory will be required to meet the manufacturing requirements.
2. **Product Development**. The integrated, iterative product development process will result in fewer engineering change

orders, more component standardization, and in fewer total components. This will result in the need for less inventory.

3. **Lead Time**. Lead times will be significantly reduced. As lead times are reduced the need for inventory will be reduced.

4. **Production Lot Sizes**. Production lot sizes and setup times will be significantly reduced. As production lot sizes are reduced, and as setup times are reduced, so too is the need for inventory.

5. **Uncertainty**. As uncertainty is reduced and certainty is managed, the need for inventories will be eliminated.

6. **Balance**. As balance is achieved through focused factories, continuous flow, sequential flow, and standardization, the need for inventories will be eliminated.

7. **Production and Inventory Control**. As straightforward, transparent production and inventory control systems are installed, schedules will be met and the need for inventory will be eliminated.

By reducing inventories, it will be easier for you to focus on the problems that originally created the need for them. Because excessive inventories will not exist in winning manufacturing operations, when a problem does occur, full attention will be quickly given to resolve the problem. Problems are not masked by inventory; problems will be fixed and prevented so that the operation may run according to plan. Thus, eliminating inventories will make it easier to maintain little or no inventory.

HOW NOT TO REDUCE INVENTORIES

Traditional manufacturing companies address inventory reduction the same way that many people address weight reduction: inconsistently. In many traditional manufacturing companies there is a cycle of "we must reduce inventories. . . we must improve customer service." Figure 22 shows that this cycle is never-ending. In some organizations the cycle follows the seasons. Out with the winter coats (the end of the year) comes a financial mandate that "we must reduce inventories." As the winter coats are stored (spring) comes a marketing mandate that "we must improve customer service." This folly will not exist with winning manufacturing.

The most popular methods of improperly reducing inventories are:

1. On the vendors back,
2. The shell game,
3. Management mandate,

4. Hire more expeditors, and

5. Over-management.

The following sections describe these ill-conceived scenarios.

On the Vendor's Back

One interpretation of just-in-time is to reduce raw material inventories by forcing your vendors to hold your inventories for you. Your relationship with the vendor does not change, except you force the vendor to hold your inventory.

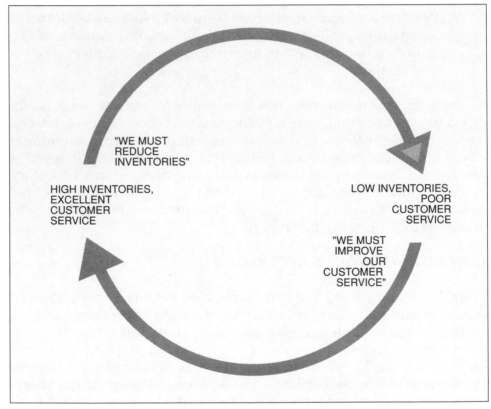

Figure 22. The traditional manufacturing
inventory reduction–customer service improvement cycle

This approach does reduce inventories but unfortunately, your vendor must increase the purchase price to pay for the storage of your raw materials. Although inventory is reduced, the total costs of manufacturing are not. Thus, reducing inventory on the back of your vendors is not a viable inventory reduction method.

The Shell Game

The shell game involves changing the status of inventories in order to give the appearance of reducing inventories. The shell game is played by establishing an inventory reduction goal for one category of inventory and then shifting inventory out of the category.

The shell game can be played with raw material by releasing excess stock to the floor. This will reduce raw material inventory, but work-in-process inventories will increase.

The shell game can also be played with raw material by creating a separate company for holding raw materials. The new company holds the raw materials until they are needed by manufacturing and released just-in-time for production. Obviously, raw material inventory is significantly reduced, but the purchase price of the raw materials increases because there really is no change in inventory quantity, just an increase in receiving costs and paperwork.

Similarly, the shell game can be played with work-in-process and finished goods by declaring inventory obsolete or by revaluing the inventory. The number of shell game possibilities is endless.

Of course, in all shell games, nothing is gained. The inventory still exists, it is just hidden under a different shell. Thus, the shell game is obviously not a viable inventory reduction method.

Management Mandate

The management-mandate scenario begins with a mandate to reduce inventory. The premise here is that if management directs that inventories be reduced, they will be reduced. The most interesting fact is that the management mandate often does appear to reduce inventories.

Once management mandates an inventory reduction, one or more of the following happens:

1. Inventory reduction on the vendors back is pursued.
2. Inventory reduction by the shell game is pursued.
3. Someone will falsify the levels of inventory.
4. The traditional manufacturing inventory reduction/improve customer service cycle will be pursued.

Typically after several months, the mandate will no longer be necessary as the inventory mandate has been achieved. Inventory levels will then return quickly to their premandate levels. Thus, the management mandate is not a viable method of reducing inventories.

Hire More Expeditors

The concept behind the hire more expeditors scenario is that if you can pursue the right priorities, the amount of inventory will be reduced. The resources needed to initiate this scenario are one expeditor and a box of red tags. For each month this approach is pursued, an additional expeditor and two additional boxes of red tags are needed.

The method will reduce inventories when first implemented. Unfortunately, the inventory reduction will not be permanent. The long-term reality is that for each lot that is expedited, another lot will be de-expedited.

The hire-more-expeditors scenario is terminated when every lot in the shop has a red tag and each expeditor is pursuing his own priorities at the expense of the companies well-being.

An interesting aspect is that just as there was a short-term inventory reduction when expeditors were placed into the shop, there will also be a short-term inventory reduction when expeditors are taken out of the shop. Inventory will stabilize at almost the same level after the expeditors are gone as before they came. The hire-more-expeditors scenario does not reduce inventories, and thus, is not a viable inventory reduction method.

Over-Management

The management-mandate scenario involved upper management. The over-management scenario involves middle management and begins when middle management decides inventories must be reduced. Middle management creates several new forms and procedures that creates a total inventory audit trail. By involving several people and conducting several meetings, the over-management scenario will be successful in reducing inventories. Unfortunately, the savings in inventories are overshadowed by the increases in overhead costs resulting from the additional middle-management involvement. The total costs of manufacturing are increased. Thus, reducing inventories by over-management is not a viable inventory reduction method.

HOW TO REDUCE INVENTORIES

The reduction of inventories begins by documenting the present levels of inventory, which should be compared to whatever industry yardsticks can be obtained. Factors to consider in determining the proper levels of inventory include industry norms, production constraints, seasonality, customer requirements, material availability, variety, and production stability.

Based upon the best information available, and the judgment of the inventory reduction team, specific inventory reduction goals should be established. An audit should be conducted for each inventory reduction goal to determine why the present level of inventory exists. This audit should be undertaken while considering all twenty Requirements of Success. While considering the goal, the audit, and the methods of how not to reduce inventories, specific approaches to reduce inventory should be identified. Economic evaluations of each approach must be conducted to certify that inventory as well as the total costs of manufacturing will be reduced.

The justifiable inventory reduction approaches must be integrated into an overall inventory reduction improvement plan. Once support for the plan is obtained it should be implemented. Results should be compared to the established goals. Once the inventory reduction goals have been accomplished, procedures must be put in place to assure the continued conformance to these goals. Only with continuous attention will acceptable inventory levels be maintained and continuous improvement be achieved.

REFERENCES

Gunn, T.G. 1987. *Manufacturing for Competitive Advantage: Becoming a World Class Manufacturer.* Ballinger Publishing Company. Cambridge, Massachusetts.

Hayes, R.H., and Wheelwright, S.C. 1984. *Restoring Our Competitive Edge: Competing Through Manufacturing.* John Wiley & Sons. New York.

Tompkins, J.A. 1985. This column may not be in time. *Industrial Product Bulletin.* May. Vol. 42, no. 5.

_____. 1987. Minimize, don't eliminate storage. *Modern Materials Handling.* December. Vol. 42, no. 12.

_____, and Cramer, M.A. 1987. Just-in-time: the real story. *CIM Technology.* August.

Chapter 12
ADAPTABILITY

MANUFACTURING FACILITIES, OPERATIONS, AND PERSONNEL MUST BECOME MORE ADAPTABLE.

Every chapter in this book has directly or indirectly referred to the need for adaptability.

- Chapter 1 explains that the basic concept of dynamic consistency requires that change be continuous. Change is described as normal, healthy and a prerequisite for progress. Continuous change requires adaptability.
- Chapter 2 describes the cost-reduction process of improve, improve, improve. This never- ending process requires adaptable facilities, operations, and personnel.
- Chapter 3 explains the reality of forecasting. Since forecasts are inherently inaccurate, manufacturing must be adaptable to meet the real-world, day-to-day fluctuations in production requirements.
- Chapter 4 describes the increased pace for product development. This pace and the requirement for manufacturing to handle a significant variety of, as yet, undefined products demand adaptable manufacturing.
- Chapter 5 stresses the requirement of being adaptable in order to be successful in the global marketplace. With this adaptability, a firm will be able to meet the customization requirement necessary to become a winning global manufacturer.
- Chapters 6 through 11 present the methodology for reducing inventories via shorter lead times, smaller lot sizes, shorter setup times, less uncertainty, greater balance, and more responsive production and inventory control systems. Maintaining the required high level of customization while providing quality customer service and low inventories may only be accomplished via adaptable manufacturing.

Therefore, the Requirement of Success that manufacturing facilities, operations, and personnel must become more adaptable is not surprising. However, what may be surprising is the confusion that results from attempting to clarify what is meant by adaptable manufacturing. Adaptable manufacturing has different meanings to different organizations and even to different people within the same organization.

The most popular definition of adaptable is the ability to become suitable for a new use. In manufacturing, *adaptable* is the ability to produce different manufacturing requirements. Herein lies the confusion; there are two different perspectives on being adaptable.

Production requirements may differ by changing what is to be produced or the volumes of what is to be produced. Flexible manufacturing is required to address changes in what is to be produced. Modular manufacturing is required to address changes in the volumes of what is to be produced. Although flexibility and modularity are both forms of adaptability, they are totally different.

The clearest definition of *flexibility* is the ability to handle a variety of requirements without being altered. Flexible manufacturing operations are those able to produce a variety of different products without altering the manufacturing operation.

On the other hand, *modularity* is defined as the ability to expand or contract without altering the approach. Modular manufacturing operations are those able to produce more or less of a product without altering the manufacturing approach.

Adaptability has to do with being flexible, modular, or both. Winning manufacturing must be adaptable, flexible, and modular.

FLEXIBILITY

Manufacturing must become more flexible. Flexible manufacturing requires focused factories, small production lot sizes, versatile equipment, and multiskilled employees.

The design, specification, and implementation of versatile manufacturing equipment are required to achieve flexible manufacturing. Equipment should be selected with sufficient versatility to handle today's manufacturing requirements and when justifiable, future requirements. Flexibility beyond today's requirements should be pursued when added long-term, beneficial flexibility can be obtained for a small incremental increase in investment.

Consider the selection of a robot as an example. Model 11D is sufficient for a specific application. However, for an increase in investment of 2 percent, model 14D can be installed. Model 14D has the same operating characteristics as a model 11D, but has 30 percent more lifting capacity. Although model 14D is not economically justifiable given today's requirements, management decided for model 14D by rationalizing that for only a 2 percent incremental expenditure, the greater capability of 14D would result in a long-term, economic benefit. This type of rationalization should be considered in the design, specification, and implementation of all manufacturing equipment. Similar consideration should be given to:

1. Adjustable length, width and depth equipment,
2. Variable speed, rate, and volume equipment, and
3. Future computer hardware and software considerations.

At the same time, you must be careful in preventing the promise of future capabilities that will waste funds today. Flexibility must be pursued, with the understanding there is a cost involved, but there is no formula or methodology that will define the proper investment to be made for flexibility. Only your judgment and experience will allow you to determine what level of investment in flexibility today will result in an adequate future return on investment.

The fourth winning manufacturing flexibility requirement is the need for multiskilled personnel. Overly restrictive work rules, excessive job classifications and labor grades, and insufficient training have often resulted in single-skilled personnel.

Winning manufacturing companies will improve speed, efficiency, and quality through multiskilling. National Steel has consolidated seventy-eight job classifications into sixteen and has broadened personnel responsibilities and participation in operations and planning. Multiskilling has resulted in National Steel's increase in speed, efficiency, quality, and profits.

Winning manufacturing companies have found multiskilling to be beneficial in identifying and solving quality problems. Since multiskilling eliminates barriers between tasks, workers better understand the implications of their performance. Personnel are better able to detect flaws in each other's work and, because of their increased visibility, solve problems more effectively. At General Motors' Detroit Gear and Axle plant, multiskilled workers were able to cut suspension warranty costs by 400 percent in two years. At Motorola, the defect rate on cellular telephones fell 77 percent in three years due to cross-trained personnel.

The approach used at Toyota Motor Corporation to develop multiskilled personnel is a three-phased job rotation program. The first phase involves each production supervisor rotating through each job within their responsibility to prove their abilities. The second phase is the rotation of all department personnel through each job in the department for on-the-job training. The third phase is the scheduling of the new multiskilled workers through all department jobs each day or week. This approach of job rotation results in:

1. Cross-trained personnel who can perform several functions,
2. Improved personnel attitudes,
3. Less fatigue and boredom,
4. Fewer accidents,
5. Better personnel communications, and
6. Improved personnel involvement with the operation's big picture.

Although this job rotation approach may be difficult to implement, the concept has considerable merit and demonstrates one method for obtaining flexible personnel.

MODULARITY

Manufacturing facilities, operations, and personnel must become more modular, which requires modular facilities, modular focused departments, and use of time modularity.

Modular facilities must be able to gracefully handle changes in production volumes. Figure 23 illustrates the continuous evolution of manufacturing facilities.

The rate of change of manufacturing facilities will increase as:

1. The rate of change in product development increases, and
2. The cost of renovations decreases.

For example, in an electronics manufacturing operation where the rate of change in the product development is very rapid and the assembly work is done on portable assembly benches, the rate of facility change is rapid. Facility changes will occur almost every day. On the other hand, in a steel mill, the time required to make one revolution of the facility life cycle could easily be ten to twenty years.

Figure 24 illustrates the four most common approaches to facility expansion. Of these, the spine approach maximizes facility modularity. Each focused factory in a spine layout may be independently expanded without affecting other focused factories.

As illustrated by the spine facility given in Figure 25 by locating all facility services, all material handling between focused factories, and all network communications in the spine, the disruption to the

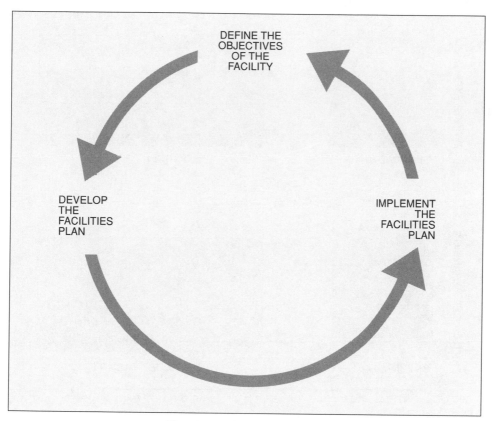

Figure 23. Facilities life cycle

facility during expansion is minimized. Distributed receiving and shipping are accommodated by locating all focused factories on exterior walls. By consolidating all material movements into the spine, it will be easier to justify automated material handling systems. The automated material handling systems will link with automatic identification traffic cops to control all materials entering and leaving the focused departments. These traffic cops, when integrated with the network communication system, provide total control of materials. The spine within the facility functions much like the spinal column in a human being; it integrates the circulatory (material handling) and nervous (communication) systems.

The second requirement of modularity is modular focused departments, which can be established by laying out the departments to accommodate modular job assignments. The key to establishing modular job assignments is to avoid trapping workers within inefficient work confines.

For example, consider a ten-person focused department. Mathematically, if 20 percent more or 20 percent less production was

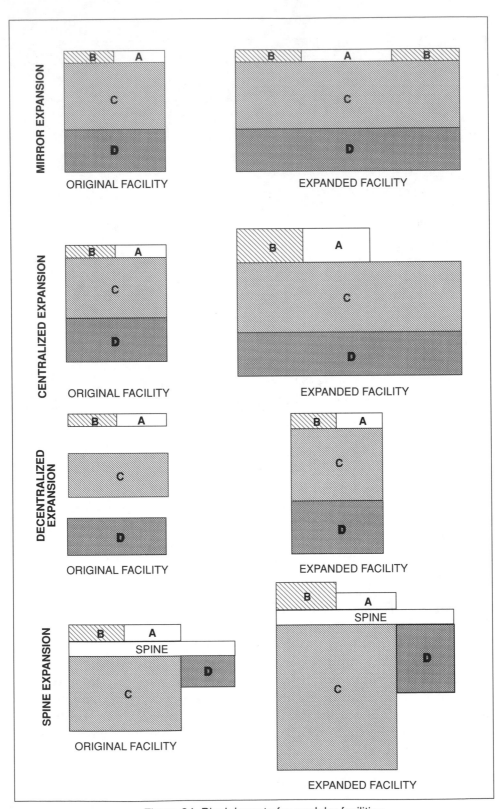

Figure 24. Block layouts for modular facilities

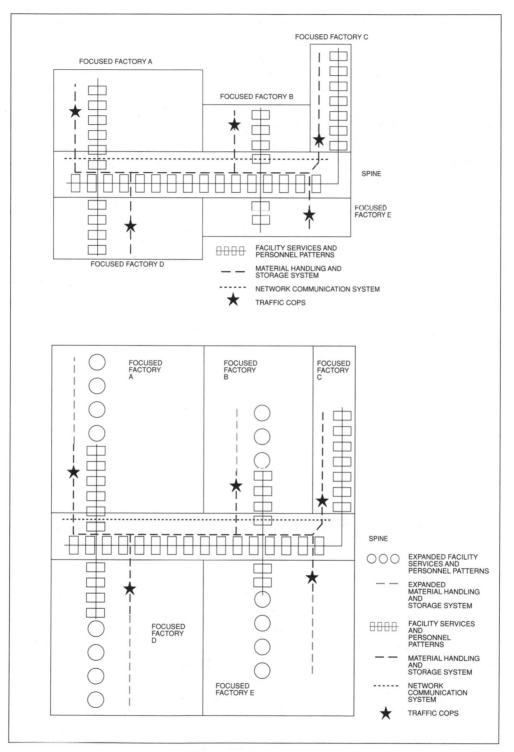

Figure 25. Illustration of a spine facility

required, twelve or eight people, respectively, would be required to meet the adjusted production levels. Unfortunately, because the production layout traps several operators, the job assignments must be made such that the mathematical answers of twelve and eight are not feasible. In fact, for this particular situation, an increase in production of 20 percent would require not twelve people, but seventeen people, and a reduction of 20 percent would require not eight people, but still the full ten operators. This is an illustration of a layout that offers no adaptability in job assignments, and thus, lacks modularity.

To the contrary, in the example in Figure 26 all employees are multiskilled. The twelve-operation focused department may operate at a production rate of 15, 30, 45, 60, 72, 90, and 120 parts per hour. Table 13 presents the job assignments for each of these production rates. Due to the layout of the modular focused department, no operators are trapped and excellent modularity exists by simply changing work assignments.

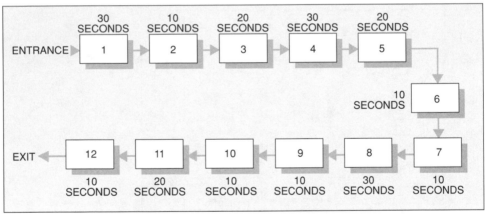

Figure 26. Modular focused department

The third topic of modularity is time modularity. Creativity in employee work schedules can have a significant impact on an operation's output. For example, a focused factory produces at a rate of 100 parts per hour. At least in theory, the maximum output in a week would be 16,800 parts per week. This would require 24-hour, seven-day-a-week production. The maximum output from one eight-hour shift, five-day-per-week operation would be 4,000 parts per week. However, if the one shift consists of seven hours of work, thirty minutes of lunch and two fifteen-minute breaks, the five-day work week would only produce 3,500 parts per week. If relief personnel maintained the operation during breaks but not lunch, the five-day work week would result in production of 3,750 parts. Thus, using time modularity can significantly change production outputs.

TABLE 13
Job Assignment For Modular Focused Factory

PRODUCTION RATE	NUMBER OF OPERATORS	OPERATOR	JOB ASSIGNMENTS	TRAVEL TIME PLUS IDLE TIME PER CYCLE
15 per hr.	1	#1	1-2-3-4-5-6-7-8-9-10-11-12	30 seconds
30 per hr.	2	#1 #2	1-2-3-10-11-12 4-5-6-7-8-9	20 seconds 10 seconds
45 per hr.	3	#1 #2 #3	1-2-11-12 3-4-9-10 5-6-7-8	10 seconds 10 seconds 10 seconds
60 per hr.	4	#1 #2 #3 #4	1-2-12 3-10-11 4-5-9 6-7-8	10 seconds 10 seconds 0 seconds 10 seconds
72 per hr.	5	#1 #2 #3 #4 #5	1-12 2-10-11 3-4 5-6-7 8-9	10 seconds 10 seconds 0 seconds 10 seconds 10 seconds
90 per hr.	6	#1 #2 #3 #4 #5 #6	1 2-11-12 3-10 4 5-6-7 8-9	10 seconds 0 seconds 10 seconds 10 seconds 0 seconds 0 seconds
120 per hr.	8	#1 #2 #3 #4 #5 #6 #7 #8	1 2-12 3-9 10-11 4 5 6-7 8	0 seconds 10 seconds 0 seconds 0 seconds 0 seconds 10 seconds 10 seconds 0 seconds

HOW TO ACHIEVE MANUFACTURING ADAPTABILITY

Fixed rules or methods to achieve adaptable manufacturing do not exist. The level of flexibility and modularity that is appropriate for your operation can only be determined by applying your judgment and experience.

The adaptability Requirement of Success for winning manufacturing does not result in a listing of principles or guidelines. To the contrary, the task of winning manufacturing adaptability is to identify and destroy artificial barriers to flexible, modular manufacturing. These barriers should come down during the planning, design, and operation of winning manufacturing factories. The question that must be asked repeatedly in winning manufacturing operations is, "Has adaptability fully and completely been taken into consideration and have all artificial barriers to adaptability been removed?"

The process of achieving winning manufacturing for adaptability should pursue the following steps:

1. Assess the adaptability of present plans, designs, and ongoing operations. Identify artificial barriers to flexibility and modularity.
2. Identify flexibility and modularity requirements. Establish specific goals for each of these requirements.
3. Identify alternative approaches to achieving the specific flexibility and modularity goals.
4. Evaluate the alternative approaches.
5. Specify the approaches that will best achieve the flexibility and modularity goals. Define an improvement plan for achieving these goals.
6. Obtain support for the improvement plan.
7. Implement the plan.
8. Audit results and further identify artificial barriers to flexibility and modularity.

REFERENCES

Alster, N., 1989. What flexible workers can do. *Fortune.* February 13.

Monden, Y. 1983. *Toyota Production System.* Industrial Engineering and Management Press. Norcross, Georgia.

Taylor, A. III. 1987. Who's ahead in the world auto world. *Fortune.* November 9. Vol. 116, no. 13.

Tompkins, J.A. 1980. Modularity and flexibility: dealing with future shock in facilities design. *Industrial Engineering.* September. Vol. 12, no. 9.

_____. 1988. You can be certain about uncertainty. *Industrial Product Bulletin.* May. Vol. 45, no. 5.

_____, and Spain, J.C. 1987. Utilization of spine concept maximizes modularity in facilities planning. *Industrial Engineering.* March. Vol. 119, no. 3.

_____, and White, J.A. 1984. *Facilities Planning.* John Wiley & Sons. New York.

Chapter 13
QUALITY

PRODUCT QUALITY, VENDOR QUALITY, AND INFORMATION QUALITY
MUST IMPROVE.

The most popular manufacturing topic of the last five years has been quality. Likewise, the most popular conference, book, and magazine article theme has also been quality. Books on quality are on the best-seller lists. Companies have adopted a wide variety of slogans and campaigns to stress the importance of quality. Companies have adopted quality as a strategic marketing theme and have spent hundreds of millions of dollars advertising their products' quality. All of these efforts, in addition to Gallup surveys, articles in nonmanu-facturing books, magazines, newspapers, and television documentaries, have given virtually every person in every developed nation an awareness of the quality issue.

The interest in quality has gone so far that the American Society of Quality Control has a sixteen-page catalog offering "Quality First" pens, pencils, rulers, letter openers, pads, sweaters, shirts, jackets, caps, buttons, lapel pins, patches, knives, belt buckles, luggage tags, playing cards, clocks, mugs, coasters, glasses, bowls, neckties, plaques, calendars, bumper stickers, card cases, charms, flash-lights, calculators, folders, paperweights, posters, brochures, gar-ment bags, flags, and even "Q" paper clips.

On Broadway, comedienne Lily Tomlin, in her one-woman play, *The Search for Signs of Intelligent Life in the Universe*, asked the audience this question: "If all manufacturing companies eliminated the quality control function, would quality run rampant?" The audience, certainly not restricted to manufacturing managers, loved the question and laughed so loudly that Lily had to pause in order for her next line to be heard.

Quality is more than a fad, more than a movement. Quality has become a crusade. Nevertheless, quality remains somewhat of a mystery. Everyone is in favor of quality; everyone talks about quality;

everyone recognizes quality when they see it. But, many find its definition unclear, its measurement elusive, and their role with respect to it uncertain. It is time for less crusading, less hype, and more understanding of quality.

UNDERSTANDING QUALITY

The most consistent definition of quality in Japan is satisfying the customer. The most consistent definition of quality in the United States is the conformance to requirements.

The Japanese definition is good because it defines the customer as the judge of quality, but it is weak because it does not lead to a method for evaluating quality. The United States' definition offers a method of evaluating quality, but its weakness is that it does not state that quality can only be obtained when the customer establishes the requirements.

The combination of the Japanese and the American definitions leads to the best definition of quality: Quality is the conformance to customer requirements.

David Garvin, in his book *Managing Quality: The Strategic and Competitive Edge*, presents the following elements of quality for which a customer's requirements should be recorded, using a car as an example:

1. **Performance.** The operating characteristics of the product (acceleration of a car)
2. **Features.** Secondary characteristics that supplement the product's operating characteristics (air conditioning in a car)
3. **Reliability.** The anticipated failure rate of the product (length of time to the failure of a car's starter)
4. **Conformance.** The lack of defects in the product when delivered (fitting of the trunk, hood, and doors of the car when delivered)
5. **Durability**. The useful life of the product (number of years before a car deteriorates to the point where it should no longer be repaired)
6. **Serviceability**. The ability to obtain satisfactory repair (availability of engine parts and ease of installation of these parts)
7. **Aesthetics**. The customer's feelings about the appearance of the product (how the customer views the styling of the car)
8. **Perceived quality**. The customer's overall feeling about the product (subjective judgment of the customer as to which is the best car)

Customer requirements should be established for each of these eight elements. The product that best conforms to these requirements is the highest-quality product.

In order to understand quality, you must understand the terms quality control, quality assurance, and total quality control. These terms are not synonymous. *Quality control* is the design of the product and processes so that the conformance of the product to customer requirements is achieved. Two principles of quality control that must be understood are:

1. Quality cannot be inspected into a product,
2. Quality cannot be built into a product.

Quality can only be designed into the product and the processes that produce it.

Quality assurance is not the design of products or processes, but the ongoing activity that ensures products conform to customer requirements. Therefore, quality control is a design activity that occurs before production, and quality assurance is an auditing activity that takes place during production.

The combination of quality control and quality assurance is known in the United States as *total quality control* and in Japan as *company-wide quality control*. For all products, first the proper design must occur to control quality and then manufacturing processes must be audited to assure quality. The combination of quality control and quality assurance is a Requirement of Success for winning manufacturing.

THE EVOLUTION OF QUALITY

Traditionally, quality has been an operational, reactive activity, not a management issue. The primary objective was for quality inspectors to travel throughout manufacturing to sort the good ones from the bad ones. Everyone knew it was unacceptable to ship bad ones, so the inspector's job was to audit manufacturing. It seemed that manufacturing management had as an objective product shipment, and quality inspectors had as an objective the legalistic application of standards to delay shipments. Not surprisingly, manufacturing managers and quality inspectors were bitter enemies.

Today, considerable progress has been made in the quality field. Although quality is often driven from the top through slogans and elaborate campaigns, quality control and quality assurance are mostly proactive. Inspectors still travel throughout the operation, but now are more sophisticated statistically and technically. Inspections are done not only to sort good ones from bad ones but much more importantly, to feed statistical process control.

Statistical process control is a management tool to bring and maintain processes in control. The proper use of statistical process control allows you to identify process variability due to assignable causes, and thus, serves as an early warning system for producing unacceptable parts. Through the use of statistical process control, the costs of poor quality may be minimized and quality may be ensured.

Quality will continue to progress. In a winning manufacturing company quality will be:

1. Top-down driven from an awareness and commitment perspective,
2. Bottom-up driven from a measurement and reporting perspective, and
3. Customer-driven from a requirements perspective. Quality will be a proactive, strategic activity of critical importance for everyone from the president to the shop-floor worker. Slogans and campaigns will be replaced by quantifiable objectives.

Inspection will be done of all units, (no more statistical sampling) in-line on a real-time basis. Inspection will often be automated. Data will flow to real-time SPC systems for a real-time audit of the process. However, the inspection objectives will be much more than attempting to identify good ones from bad ones and data collection for SPC. By being in-line and real-time, inspection will be the hub of the following:

1. The control of the manufacturing process,
2. The reduction of variability and product tolerances; that is, increased consistency,
3. Feedback and machine calibration (automatically where automatic inspection is utilized),
4. Real-time line stoppage and the identification of the reason for stoppage (automatic line stoppage where automatic inspection is utilized),
5. Predictive maintenance,
6. Management reporting,
7. Customer quality documentation, and
8. Feedback to product and process planning.

INFORMATION QUALITY

The most popular responses to the question, "What are your company's greatest assets?" are "Our employees" and "Our customers". Of course, without either of these, there would be no company, so these are valid answers.

However, there is one other response that should be rated equally as important as employees and customers; without the asset of information, there is no company. Without information, there are no products, no customers, no orders, no materials, no machines, no personnel, no anything. It is quality information that makes a company function.

The definition of quality information is accurate data organized in accordance with the requirements of the user. Even worse than no information is misinformation, the opposite of quality information. Misinformation consists of inaccurate data. If you have to choose between quality components and misinformation, or scrap components and quality information, you will always be better off with the scrap components and the quality information.

Interesting features of quality information are:

1. It can be processed at very high speeds,
2. It is reusable,
3. It costs less now than ever before, and
4. It can be made available to many sources simultaneously with the initial input.

Quality information, like vendor quality and product quality, is a Requirement of Success. Systems must be put in place to provide for accurate, reliable, consistent information. Quality control and quality assurance for information are just as important as quality control and quality assurance for vendors and products. Misinformation, like defective parts, must be found, investigated, and corrected so that the cause of the misinformation is eliminated.

HOW TO IMPROVE PRODUCT, VENDOR, AND INFORMATION QUALITY

Unfortunately, the slogan "Quality Is Free" has become quite popular. This is unfortunate because some managements have taken the stance that quality can be improved for little or no investment of time and capital. Nothing could be further from the truth. To improve quality, a significant investment of capital and of time by all levels of an organization is required. No, quality is not free; an excellent investment, but not free.

A successful quality improvement program should be a broad-based, participative effort involving upper management, middle management, purchasing, product development, engineering, marketing, supervision, shop-floor personnel, vendors, and customers. Everyone who has an impact on quality must be educated to obtain an awareness and understanding of quality.

Based on an understanding of quality, upper management must make a strong commitment to quality and communicate it to all personnel. Upper management must demonstrate the commitment through active participation and capital investment.

The understanding of quality and the commitment to quality will be the foundation for a quality improvement program. Once the foundation is in place, the following steps should be taken to improve quality:

1. **Know your customer**. Identify your customer. Understand your customer's business. Adopt your customer's perspective.

2. **Define customer requirements.** Communicate with your customers. Obtain a clear definition of your customer's requirements. Make sure all parties involved share the same customer expectations.

3. **Assess present quality performance**. Document your performance. Compare this performance to the customer requirements. Identify areas where customer expectations are not exceeded.

4. **Identify problems**. Investigate performance shortfalls. Define the reasons for them. Communicate with all parties involved to understand the shortfalls.

5. **Specify alternative solutions**. Break through communication barriers and traditional constraints to identify creative potential solutions. Be certain that for each alternative solution, the problems are solved and not just relocated. Document the operating characteristics of each alternative solution. Verify that each alternative solution will result in exceeding customer requirements.

6. **Evaluate alternative solutions**. Do an economic and qualitative evaluation of each alternative solution. Identify the best solution to each performance shortfall.

7. **Establish improvement plans.** Translate the selected solutions into an action plan. Obtain support for the action plan.

8. **Implement improvement plans**. Install equipment, train personnel, and debug the installation of the solution. Assure solution's performance.

9. **Audit results**. Verify that performance exceeds customer expectations. Install systems to assure ongoing exceeding of customer requirements.

REFERENCES

Dingus, V.R., and Golomski, W.A. (Eds.) 1988. *A Quality Revolution in Manufacturing*. Industrial Engineering and Management Press. Norcross, Georgia.

Dreyfuss, J. 1988. Victories in the quality crusade. *Fortune.* October 10. Vol. 118, no. 8.

Monden, Y. 1983. *Toyota Production System.* Industrial Engineering and Management Press. Norcross, Georgia.

Mullins, P. 1987. European quality production. *Production.* December. Vol. 99, No. 12.

Schonberger, R.J. 1986. *World Class Manufacturing.* Free Press. New York.

Sherman, W.H. 1988. Inspection: do we need it? *Manufacturing Engineering.* May. Vol. 100, No. 5.

Vasilash, G.S. 1988. Buried treasure and other benefits of quality. *Production.* March. Vol. 100, No. 3.

Wallach, S.L. 1987. The new look in statistical process control. *Managing Automation.* December. Vol. 2, No. 12.

Waterman, R.H. 1987. *The Renewal Factor: How To Best Get and Keep The Competitive Edge.* Bantam Books. New York.

Winter, R.E. 1987. Upgrading of factories replaces the concept of total automation. *Wall Street Journal.* November 30.

Yanecek, F. 1988. Working inventory wonders. *Transportation and Distribution.* May. Vol. 29, no. 5.

Chapter 14
MAINTENANCE

MANUFACTURING PROCESS FAILURES MUST BE MINIMIZED.

In many manufacturing organizations, the maintenance function does not receive proper respect. The naive perception is that maintenance does not add value to a product, and thus, the best maintenance is the least-cost maintenance. Armed with this false perception, traditional manufacturing companies have:

1. Under emphasized preventive, corrective and routine maintenance,
2. Not addressed predictive maintenance,
3. Not properly trained maintenance personnel, and
4. Not properly developed maintenance management.

Excessive, unpredictable manufacturing process failures have been the result.

Maintenance is not an insurance policy or a security blanket; it is a Requirement of Success. Without effective maintenance, machines and systems will fail. When failure occurs:

1. Certainty will not be achieved and uncertainty will be the norm. This is contrary to the Requirement of Success that uncertainty must be minimized.
2. Balance will not be obtainable. This is contrary to the Requirement of Success that all operations must be balanced.
3. Inventories will be required. This is contrary to the Requirement of Success that inventories must be reduced.

Winning manufacturing operations cannot tolerate manufacturing process failures. To minimize such failures, maintenance must become an important management priority.

MANUFACTURING MAINTENANCE

Manufacturing maintenance has five levels. These are:

Level I: Breakdown Maintenance
Level II: Routine Maintenance
Level III: Corrective Maintenance
Level IV: Preventive Maintenance
Level V: Predictive Maintenance

Maintenance in traditional manufacturing companies has been focused on Level I. Maintenance in winning manufacturing companies will focus on Levels V, IV, III and II, in an attempt to minimize Level I maintenance.

Breakdown maintenance (Level I) is the repair of equipment or systems after they have failed. It is unplanned, undesirable, expensive, and usually avoidable if the other levels of maintenance are performed effectively.

Routine maintenance (Level II) is lubrication, tool changing, and proactive repair. Lubrication should be done on a regular schedule. Tool changing should take place either on a regular schedule or based upon a higher level of maintenance that identifies the need for a tool change. Proactive repair is a machine or system repair that is done based upon a higher level of maintenance determining that if the repair does not take place, a breakdown will occur.

Corrective maintenance (Level III) is the adjusting or calibrating of the machine or system. Corrective maintenance will be undertaken to improve either the quality or the performance of a machine or system. The need for corrective maintenance will be the result of predictive or preventive maintenance or from statistical process control.

Preventive maintenance (Level IV) includes periodic inspection, waste removal, and general housekeeping. It is a continuous process whose objective is to minimize future maintenance problems.

Predictive maintenance (Level V) predicts potential problems by sensing the operations of a machine or system. This level monitors operations, diagnoses undesirable trends, and pinpoints potential problems. In its simplest form, an operator hearing a change in the sound made by the equipment or system predicts a potential problem, which leads to either corrective or routine maintenance. Similarly, a predictive maintenance expert system can monitor machine vibrations. By gathering vibration data and analyzing this data in accordance to normal operating conditions, the expert system is able to predict and pinpoint the cause of a potential problem.

An important winning manufacturing issue is the determination of who should perform each level of maintenance. Traditional manufacturing has most often taken the approach that operators operate and maintenance people maintain. This traditional view is wrong. In winning manufacturing, it is important to give operators a sense of ownership. A critical aspect of this is to make the operator responsible for as much machine or system maintenance as possible. Once the operator accepts ownership, the operator will want to learn more about the machine or system's operation, take personal interest in the cleanliness and orderliness of the machine or system, and take responsibility for the machine or system's performance.

In winning manufacturing operations where operators are present, they should be responsible for all of Level V, IV, and III maintenance operations and as much Level II maintenance as is practical. The level of practicality should be determined by the complexity of the machines or systems and the competency of the operators.

In winning manufacturing operations where the operators have been replaced by automotation, maintenance personnel should be assigned to specific machines or systems, establish the machine or system ownership, and perform all five levels of maintenance.

WINNING MANUFACTURING MAINTENANCE

In addition to transferring many of the maintenance activities to the operators, the following principles of winning manufacturing maintenance should be pursued:

1. **Reliability**. More reliable machines and systems will be specified, installed, and used.
2. **Redundancy**. Critical machines and systems will have backups provided so that if something fails, a secondary machine or system will take over.
3. **Modularity**. All machines and systems will be modularly designed so that any failure can be repaired quickly.
4. **Obsolescence**. The replacement of machines and systems will be closely monitored and managed.
5. **Maintenance personnel**. A significant upgrade in the level of personnel involved with maintenance will take place.
6. **Maintenance training and education**. Maintenance training and education will be computer based, self-paced, and continually upgraded.
7. **Expert systems**. Computer-controlled machines and systems will be specified with expert system predictive maintenance systems, or at least, with the capability of adding the expert system later.

8. **Working environment**. Winning manufacturing operations will be clean and orderly, and good housekeeping will be maintained.
9. **Maintenance management**. The quality of the maintenance function will significantly improve, because computerized maintenance management systems will encompass the total maintenance function.
10. **Maintenance data base**. Machines and systems will be fully documented when installed. This documentation, in conjunction with the operating history, will form a maintenance data base that will serve as the foundation for the management of the maintenance function.
11. **Maintenance storeroom**. The spare-parts storeroom will be orderly, space efficient, labor efficient, responsive, and effective.
12. **Maintenance inventory**. The proper quantity of the proper spare parts will be on hand to support an effective maintenance function.
13. **Maintenance and engineering**. Maintenance and engineering will work closely during systems specification, installation, startup and operation to provide maintenance with the technical depth required to maintain all machines and systems.
14. **Maintenance profession**. The profession of maintenance will be viewed as a key profession for success in winning manufacturing operations.

HOW TO MINIMIZE MANUFACTURING PROCESS FAILURE

Manufacturing process failures will be minimized in a winning manufacturing company by the following three-phase maintenance improvement process:

Phase I: Management Commitment to Maintenance
Phase II: Establish Maintenance Function
Phase III: Manage Maintenance Function

Unless management is committed to maintenance, manufacturing process failures will not be minimized. Phase I is the foundation upon which manufacturing process failure minimization is based. The steps of Phase I are:

1. Educate upper management on the importance of maintenance to winning manufacturing.
2. Obtain upper management's commitment to effective manufacturing maintenance.

3. Communicate upper management's commitment to maintenance to the entire manufacturing organization.
4. Appoint a highly qualified manager to the position of manufacturing maintenance champion.
5. Mandate that all new machines and systems will have the
active involvement of maintenance during planning, design,
specification, selection, and implementation.

The manufacturing maintenance champion should build upon
management's commitment to maintenance by proceeding with the
following Phase II steps:

1. Document the present maintenance organization, staffing, facilities, equipment, and procedures.
2. Establish or upgrade existing maintenance data base. Each
machines or system's maintenance data base should include:
    a) Machine or system identification,
    b) Manufacturer or supplier,
    c) Capacity,
    d) Drawings,
    e) Parts list,
    f) Manufacturer maintenance specifications, and
    g) Maintenance record.
3. Evaluate present maintenance function. Are the right people
performing the right work in order to obtain the right results?
Identify specific maintenance problems. Specify mean times
between process failures and the duration of downtime. Assess
all five levels of maintenance for each machine or system.
4. Define who should perform each level of maintenance for each
machine or system.
5. Evaluate present personnel and facilities to perform the maintenance established in Step 4. Identify personnel qualification
problems and facility problems.
6. Develop maintenance training and education programs for operators and maintenance personnel. Implement these programs.
7. Plan, design, specify, purchase, and implement required maintenance facilities and equipment.
8. Establish upgraded maintenance standard operating procedures for all five levels of maintenance. Implement these
procedures.

Phase III of winning manufacturing maintenance is the management of the function established in Phase II. The steps in this phase
follow:

1. Maintain maintenance data base.
2. Review machinery and system obsolescence.
3. Participate in new machinery and system planning, design, specification, selection, and implementation.
4. Update training and education of all operators and maintenance personnel.
5. Follow maintenance standard operating procedures.
6. Identify maintenance problems and correct them.

REFERENCES

Gunn, T.G. 1987. *Manufacturing for Competitive Advantage: Becoming a World Class Manufacturer.* Ballinger Publishing Company. Cambridge, Massachusetts.

Hayes, R.M., and Wheelwright, S.C. 1984. *Restoring Our Competitive Edge: Competing Through Manufacturing.* John Wiley & Sons. New York.

Katzel, J. 1987. Applying predictive maintenance. *Plant Engineering.* June 18. Vol. 41, no. 12.

Lewis, B.T., and Marron, J.P. Eds. 1973. *Facilities and Plant Engineering Handbook.* McGraw-Hill. New York.

Macaulay, S. 1988. Amazing things can happen if you keep it clean. *Production.* May. Vol. 100, no. 5.

Piper, J. 1987. Training for advanced technology. *Plant Engineering.* June 18. Vol. 41, no. 12.

Salvendy, G. Ed.1982. *Handbook of Industrial Engineering.* John Wiley & Sons. New York. Ch. 11.7.

Schonberger, R.J. 1986. *World Class Manufacturing.* Free Press. New York.

Tompkins, J.A., and Smith, J.D. Eds. 1988. *The Warehouse Management Handbook.* McGraw-Hill. New York.

Chapter 15
MATERIAL FLOW

MATERIAL FLOW MUST BE EFFICIENT.

In order to define the material flow through your operation, you must define the material and the flow. To understand the material, you must understand what is moving; to understand the flow, you must understand where and when something is moving. If you know the what, where and when of a move, you then know the material flow requirements.

The design of the material handling system is based on the material flow requirements. If you know the material and the flow, you can design the material handling system method; then you know the how and who of the material handling system. Figure 27 illustrates this relationship between the material flow requirements and the material handling system.

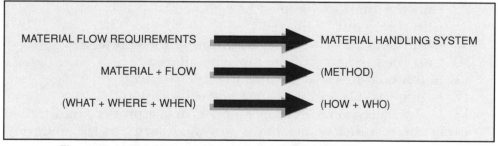

Figure 27. Material flow requirements for material handling systems

A major problem in traditional manufacturing is that material handling systems are being designed based upon such obsolete specifications of material flow requirements as long lead times, large production lots, high levels of inventory, nonfocused departments, and nonfocused factories. A properly designed material handling system based upon obsolete requirements will result in efficient material handling systems that are performing the wrong material flows. In winning manufacturing, the emphasis must first be put on establishing the correct material flow requirements and then, and only then, should the material handling system be designed.

WINNING MANUFACTURING AND MATERIAL HANDLING SYSTEMS DESIGN

An essential ingredient in designing a winning manufacturing material handling system is to separate the winning and traditional material flow requirements. The best method of determining the winning manufacturing material flow requirements is through the liberal use of the question "why?" The insertion of "why?" in the material flow equation presented in Figure 27 results in:

$$[WHY (WHAT + WHERE + WHEN)] =====> (HOW + WHO)$$

The multiplication of the WHAT + WHERE + WHEN by WHY indicates the need to ask the following questions for each material flow requirement:

1. Can the move be eliminated?
2. Can the move be combined with another move?
3. Can the move be simplified?
4. Can the sequence of moves be changed?
5. Can the unit load be changed?
6. Can the material be packaged differently?
7. Can the quantity handled be reduced?
8. Can the layout be altered?
9. Can the move be done as a portion of the operation?
10. Can the frequency of the move be altered?
11. Is material received in the correct location?
12. Is material shipped from the correct location?
13. Is the material received or shipped in the proper quantity?
14. Is there sufficient flexibility and modularity in the material flow requirements?
15. Is a change in the process going to take place?
16. Are alternative routings properly considered?
17. Are future changes going to impact the material flow requirements?
18. Are there exceptions that need to be considered?

19. Are there sensitive or unusual aspects of the material to be moved?
20. Are there special move requirements that need to be taken into consideration?

While each of these questions is being asked, the summation over all moves should occur. This summation indicates the integration of the methods for each move into a material handling system. The inclusion of this summation results in the following winning manufacturing material flow equation:

$$\sum_{\text{MOVES}} [\text{WHY} \ (\text{WHAT} + \text{WHERE} + \text{WHEN})] =====> (\text{HOW} + \text{WHO})$$

However, a questioning attitude may not be enough. The remaining traditional manufacturing roadblocks are the following obsolete material handling system design guidelines:

1. The best material handling is no material handling.
2. The shorter the distance traveled, the better the flow.
3. Straight-line material flow paths are best.
4. Handle all loads in as large a unit load as possible.

The following subsections present why these traditional guidelines are obsolete.

The Best Material Handling Is No Material Handling

If this guideline is interpreted as "Why perform this move?" the guideline is healthy and should be pursued. What is unhealthy, and in fact dangerous, is when this guideline is interpreted as, "Since the best material handling is no material handling, I need not be concerned with material handling." Many traditional companies adopt this unhealthy interpretation: no one plans material handling systems, no one budgets for an investment in them, and therefore, the only ones that are installed are afterthoughts. This does not result in winning manufacturing.

The Shorter The Distance Traveled, The Better The Flow

Of course, if given the choice of moving a load twenty feet or moving the same load forty feet by the same method, the twenty-foot move is preferable. However, if given the choice of moving a load manually twenty feet or moving the same load forty feet on an economically justified automated material handling system, the forty-foot move is probably desirable. Yes, the distance traveled is an issue, but it is not the entire issue. Would you rather walk 200 miles or fly in a plane 2,000 miles? Although 2,000 miles is further, much less effort and time is involved with flying the distance. The real issue is not how far; the real issue is which material handling method results in the least total cost of manufacturing. The winning manufacturing material handling system can be designed only by evaluating the total costs of manufacturing.

Straight-Line Material Flow Paths Are Best

Much like the shorter travel distance guideline, this guideline is only valid for the most trivial of examples. In reality, the straightness of a flow path has nothing to do with winning manufacturing. For example: Would you prefer a move of thirty feet that was straight or a move of eighteen feet that had an irregular flow path? The question is absurd. Winning manufacturing is concerned with reducing the total costs of manufacturing, not the straightness of a flow path.

Handle All Loads In As Large A Unit Load As Practical

Once again, this guideline as a general principle may have some merit. It certainly is a good decision to go to the pizza store once for two pizzas as opposed to making two separate trips for one pizza per trip. However, pizza is not the same as a material handling issue. To move a large unit load requires the acceptance of large production lot sizes, a large piece of material handling equipment, and large amounts of space.

If a pallet of parts is to be moved by a fork lift, an automated guided vehicle system, or a pallet conveyor, large amounts of either aisle or overhead space will be required. A cost-saving alternative is to break the pallet into a number of smaller unit loads and convey them on a smaller, less expensive conveyor. The smaller unit load will allow for more responsive, less expensive, and less space consuming material handling systems.

It is not true that the largest practical load should always be handled; what should be handled is the load that results in the lowest total cost of manufacturing.

CONTINUOUS-FLOW MANUFACTURING

Discrete-flow manufacturing is characterized by the infrequent movement of large unit loads. Continuous-flow manufacturing is characterized by the frequent movement of small unit loads.

Guidelines for facilitating continuous-flow manufacturing include:

1. Standardize unit loads and material handling equipment to facilitate efficient, effective, and reliable material handling systems.
2. Eliminate, whenever possible, intermediate material handling steps between two consecutive points of use by tying operations together.
3. Minimize the number of material handling steps between two consecutive points of use.
4. Combine the material handling step with the processing step so that the exit from one operation most conveniently feeds the input to the next operation.
5. When manual material handling is most economical, minimize the amount of manual activity by minimizing walking, travel distances, and motions.
6. Eliminate manual handling by mechanizing or automating material handling whenever economically justified.
7. Review all floor space and overhead space for effective utilization.
8. Integrate material flow and information flow whenever feasible.
9. Integrate the flow of materials from distributed receiving to focused factories, through focused departments, to other focused factories, to distributed shipping into one material handling system.
10. Be creative in establishing the most adaptable, maintainable, and responsive material handling system.

HOW TO ESTABLISH EFFICIENT MATERIAL FLOW

A winning manufacturing material handling system should not be designed until you have established winning manufacturing material flow requirements by reducing lead times, production lots, and inventory, and establishing focused departments and focused factories. Until these Requirements of Success are implemented, any attempt to create a winning manufacturing material handling system will be futile. Once these Requirements of Success are implemented, an efficient material handling system should be designed by pursuing the following steps:

1. Define the objectives and the scope of the material handling system.
2. Establish the material flow requirements. Verify that these requirements are consistent with winning manufacturing.

3. Generate alternative material handling system designs for meeting the material flow requirements.
4. Evaluate alternative material handling system designs.
5. Select the preferred material handling system design.
6. Establish an improvement plan.
7. Obtain support for the improvement plan.
8. Implement the preferred material handling system.
9. Audit systems performance and refine as necessary.

REFERENCES

Hill, I.D. 1984. Modern manufacturing techniques require flexible approach to facilities planning. *Industrial Engineering*. May.

Huber, R.F. 1988. Think of it as flow. *Production*. June. Vol. 100, no. 6.

Tompkins, J.A., and White, J.A. 1984. *Facilities Planning*. John Wiley & Sons. New York.

Chapter 16
MATERIAL TRACKING AND CONTROL

MATERIAL TRACKING AND CONTROL SYSTEMS MUST BE UPGRADED.

Upgraded material tracking and control systems must be in place to achieve winning manufacturing. Otherwise, responsive, continuous-flow manufacturing cannot function.

The material tracking and control system in winning manufacturing is significantly different from the material tracking and control system in traditional manufacturing. The most significant differences are:

1. Continuous-flow winning manufacturing requires real-time, quick-response tracking and control. This differs from traditional, discrete-flow manufacturing, where batch tracking and control was acceptable.

2. The flow through winning manufacturing focused departments requires tracking only when entering or leaving the focused department. This is significantly simpler than traditional manufacturing tracking, which must occur after each operation.

3. With significantly reduced raw material inventories and the emphasis on quick customer service in winning manufacturing, vendor communications must be real-time. This significantly broadens the scope of the winning manufacturing information systems as compared to traditional manufacturing where vendor communications are often neglected, delayed, or after- the-fact.

To accommodate these differences, the upgraded material tracking and control system will be a simple, real-time system using automatic identification and electronic data interchange.

SIMPLE, REAL-TIME MATERIAL TRACKING AND CONTROL

A major difference between a winning manufacturing material tracking and control system and a traditional manufacturing material tracking and control system is the response time allowed for decisions and actions. In winning manufacturing, responses are required in minutes or seconds. In traditional manufacturing material tracking and control systems, responses of days or weeks are normal. Table 14 characterizes this response time issue.

TABLE 14
Material Tracking And Control System Response

FUNCTION	TYPICAL WINNING MANUFACTURING RESPONSE TIME	TYPICAL TRADITIONAL MANUFACTURING RESPONSE TIME
Informing vendor of schedule change	By electonic data interchange – seconds	By mailing a purchase order revision – weeks
Indentification of material receipt	By automatic identification – seconds	By cross referencing a packing slip against an open purchase order file – weeks
Incoming material inspection	By certified source inspection program – completed before shipped	By in-plant quality control inspections – days
From receipt to shop floor issue	By distributed receiving, balanced production and electronic data interchange – minutes	By raw material stockroom and order release system – weeks
From release to shop floor component completion	By small production lots and focused factories – hours	By large batch production and unfocused factories – weeks
From completion in one focused department until dispatch to next focused department	By automatic identification and continuous flow manufacturing – minutes	By shop floor information packet and batch manufacturing – days
From completed production until customer informed of completion	By automatic identification and electronic data interchange – minutes	By shipping to customer – weeks
From change in product design to implementation of corresponding change in production process	By small production lots and real-time computer control – minutes	By elaborate change order process – weeks

Figure 28 illustrates the simplicity of a winning manufacturing material tracking and control system. The vendor and shop floor schedules are the outputs of manufacturing resource planning (see Figure 20). In fact, the combination of Figure 28 and Figure 20 results in the manufacturing systems and materials management modules of computer integrated manufacturing (see Chapter 20).

AUTOMATIC IDENTIFICATION AND ELECTRONIC DATA INTERCHANGE

Automatic identification has become so widespread that virtually everyone in a developed country has written checks containing magnetic ink coding, used credit cards incorporating magnetic strips, or purchased products identified with bar codes. In addition, radio frequency, surface acoustical wave, machine vision, and voice recognition are all part of the automatic identification technology.

Unfortunately, much of what is written about automatic identification involves what I call the science of automatic identification (reflected light, resolution, depth of field, bar code symbols, printing techniques, and so on). However, the science of automatic identification is not important; understanding how to use automatic identification is. It is inaccurate and expensive for a person to identify items and accurate and inexpensive to use automatic identification to identify them.

All vendors of winning manufacturing companies will employ product coding in their production process that can also be used by the manufacturers. The same code often will be used by the manufacturer's customers.

Virtually all unit loads moved will be tracked by automatic identification, and materials received at a distributed receiving function will be automatically identified. The real-time dispatch of the materials will then be triggered. If the materials need to be stored temporarily when they arrive at the storage location, they will be automatically identified and then stored. When retrieved, they will be automatically reidentified and dispatched to a focused factory where they will be automatically identified and dispatched to the appropriate focused department. The focused department will automatically identify the material, adjust the setup, and perform the series of operations within the department. When the operations are complete, the parts will be automatically identified and properly dispatched. This process will continue until the product is finished. Whenever a part or group of parts loses its identification, a new code will be applied and the full audit trail will be carried forward. This process will permit traceability from vendor, through focused factories, to the customer, through the customer's focused factories, to the customer's customer and so on, all the way to the ultimate user.

Using automatic identification to dispatch and then receive ma-

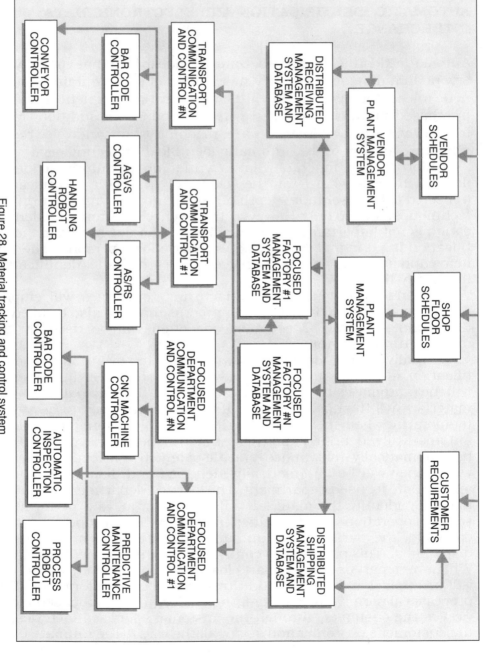

Figure 28: Material tracking and control system

terials provides for positive tracking and excellent material control. A weakness in this tracking and control process occurs when materials are transferred from vendor to customer. Instead of having a continuous tracking of materials, the information about the materials is printed on a packing list and shipped with the product. Upon receipt, the customer uses the document to begin a new tracking and control process. This is unnecessary. The proper approach is for the vendor and the customer to be integrated, just as two focused factories in a plant are integrated.

This vendor-customer integration is called Electronic Data Interchange (EDI), which is no more than treating your vendors like a remote, but integrated focused factory. Once in place, EDI eliminates the paper flow between a vendor and a customer. The customer feeds the vendor's schedule by EDI. The vendor then provides a periodic update by EDI on the status of the ordered materials. When the vendor ships the materials, EDI informs the customer. Thus, the customer does not receive unexpected goods. Automatic identification is used to receive the materials and update purchasing, accounts payable, and inventory records. There literally is no paperwork; there is simple, real-time material tracking and control instead.

HOW TO UPGRADE MATERIAL TRACKING AND CONTROL SYSTEMS

The material tracking and control system upgrade must be done in conjunction with the creation of winning manufacturing. A material tracking and control system team should be created and given the responsibility of leading the material tracking and control systems efforts. This team must work in unison with the winning manufacturing team.

For example, a prerequisite for the success of a focused winning manufacturing department will be an upgraded material tracking and control system. The most frequent problem with focused departments is a lack of coordination between the designers of the focused departments and the designers of the material tracking and control systems. This problem can be avoided by having the material tracking and control system team actively involved with the overall design of the focused department and having the focused department team actively involved with the material tracking and control system design.

Before addressing any specific upgrades to the material tracking and control system, the team must define:

1. The overall approach to material tracking and control, and
2. The overall computer system architecture.

Based upon these top-level designs, the material tracking and control system team should take the following steps to upgrade the material tracking and control system:

1. Document the present material tracking and control system. Define the present operating procedures and the computer system interfaces.
2. Establish a functional specification. In laymen's terms, explain the overall operation and the specific tasks to be performed by the upgraded material tracking and control system.
3. Within the context of the overall material tracking and control system approach and the overall computer system architecture, define alternative approaches to upgrade the material tracking and control system to accomplish the functional specification.
4. Evaluate the alternative approaches. Consider not only the economics of the alternative approaches but also the risk, reliability, modularity, flexibility, ease of installation, response time, maintainability, fail-safe position, and so on.
5. Select the best approach. Identify a pilot project to install, test, debug, and refine the updated material tracking and control system.
6. Develop a plan to implement the pilot project and a plan to implement the updated material tracking and control system.
7. Obtain support for pursuing the pilot project and the updated material tracking and control system.
8. Implement the pilot project.
9. Audit the pilot project's performance. Provide relevant feedback and make required changes.
10. Implement the upgraded material tracking and control system. Audit results to assure satisfaction of the functional specifications.

REFERENCES

Daisy, P.F. 1988. Resisting EDI could be hazardous to your firm. *Transportation and Distribution*. June. Vol. 29, no. 6.

Gould, L. 1987. Technologies for machine perception. *Managing Automation*. December. Vol. 2, no. 12.

Tompkins, J.A., and Smith, J.D. Eds. 1983. *Automated Material Handling and Storage*. Auerbach Publishers. Pennsauken, New Jersey.

Chapter 17
HUMAN RESOURCES

EVERY MANAGER MUST BE DEDICATED TO CREATING AN ENVIRONMENT WHERE EVERY EMPLOYEE IS MOTIVATED AND HAPPY.

Winning manufacturing companies will have winning employees, and winning employees will only work for winning companies. At first examination, this statement may indicate the old "which came first, the chicken or the egg?" problem; that is, how can a company become a winning company in order to attract the winning employees needed to become a winning company? The answer to this apparently unanswerable question lies in a basic fact of life: everyone is a winner.

The book *In Search of Excellence* by Peters and Waterman describes a psychological study in which a random sample of male adults was asked a series of questions. When asked about their ability to get along with others, 100 percent of the subjects put themselves in the top half of the population; 60 percent rated themselves in the top 10 percent, and 25 percent thought they were in the top 1 percent of the population. On the question of leadership, 70 percent thought of themselves as being in the top 25 percent. On the issue of athletic ability, 60 percent said they were in the top 25 percent. This led Peters and Waterman to the following conclusion:

"The message that comes through so poignantly in the studies we received is that we like to think of ourselves as winners."

Therefore, for a company to be a winning company, it should hire employees who believe they are winners, and create an environment where every employee is motivated and happy so that winners remain winners.

For a manager to create this environment, the two most important issues are:

1. Training and education, and
2. Trust.

TRAINING AND EDUCATION

It is very easy to get buried in a terminology trap with the terms *training* and *education*. Consider the following:

1. You train dogs; you educate people.
2. Training is the how; education is the why.
3. Training imparts skills; education imparts knowledge.
4. The result of training is something a person can do. The result of education is something a person has learned.
5. Training is what everyone in an organization below one's level needs. Education is what one's level and above needs.

There seems to be a status distinction with the terms training and education. This is unfortunate, as we all need both training and education to maximize our contributions to our companies.

To avoid the terminology trap and the status distinction, I shall avoid further use of the terms training and education and use the term *development* to cover both training and education. A development program that will maintain winning employees and thus result in a winning company, must address the following issues:

1. What development is needed?
2. How should this development be achieved?

WHAT DEVELOPMENT IS NEEDED?

All employees need three types of development:

1. Visionary development,
2. General development, and
3. Specific development.

Visionary development is the basic foundation upon which happy and motivated employees evolve. This foundation was called basic beliefs, the bedrocks, philosophies of business, and Requirements of Success in Chapter 1. Visionary development is the consistency portion of dynamic consistency.

All employees, from the chairman of the board to the lowest position in an organization, must understand winning manufacturing and its impact on their companies or there will be no shared beliefs, no winning employees, and no winning manufacturing companies. Therefore, the most important developmental need of every manufacturing company is for everyone in the company to understand winning manufacturing. Fulfilling this visionary development need will be a major step towards winning manufacturing. (Appendix E describes the process of winning manufacturing visionary development.)

General developmental needs are categorized as general knowledge development and general skill development. General knowledge development includes a general understanding of:

1. How your company is organized,
2. The technology involved with your manufacturing operations,
3. How your products arc used,
4. Who uses your product,
5. Your company's competition, and
6. Your company's strengths, weaknesses, opportunities, and challenges.

General skill development is the learning of skills that are needed to best contribute to a company's success. These general skills include:

1. Problem solving,
2. Planning,
3. Cost reduction,
4. Quality enhancement,
5. Communications,
6. Managing,
7. Goal setting,
8. Creativity, and
9. Computer literacy.

The challenge of general development is in determining who would benefit from which type of development. Typically, managers underestimate the value of having their employees exposed to general development. As a guideline, any developmental program of interest to a manager is probably also of interest to the manager's staff. Please keep in mind that greater understanding leads to motivation and happiness.

Specific developmental needs are programs designed for special groups of individuals. For example, computer programmers will require a specific program when a new language is installed; maintenance personnel will require one when a new machine is installed; sales personnel will require a specific developmental program when a new product is introduced; and so on.

An important issue is to avoid overly restricting the participants in the specific developmental activities. Developing employees beyond their present position will provide the benefits of multi-skilling (see Chapter 12).

HOW SHOULD THIS DEVELOPMENT BE ACHIEVED?

Development is never complete in winning companies. Retraining is a negative term. The implication of retraining is that prior training is obsolete and must be redone. The concept of it leads to the destructive question, "Can old employees be retrained?" There will be no retraining in winning companies, only the continuous development of all employees.

The basic approach to developing is to uncover, discover, and recover. The first step, uncover, means that the need must be uncovered in the mind of the person being developed. This person must believe there is a purpose in developing new knowledge or skills. Next, there must be a discovery on the part of the participant of the new knowledge or skill. The person being developed must be immersed to the point where the brain comprehends the new knowledge or skill. Lastly, during recovery, the knowledge or skill is put into practice. Only by experimenting with the knowledge or skill is the development successful. Without recovery, there is no application of the knowledge or skill and thus, no true development.

Each company should establish a program that meets the needs of the employees, and then continually update these programs. At Tompkins Associates, Inc., we utilize:

1. **Planning retreats.** Off-site, multiday planning meetings for upper management to evaluate progress and develop strategic plans.
2. **Employee retreats**. Off-site, multiday meetings for a broad cross section of employees where the vision for the company is presented, strategic plans are presented, and goals and objectives are established.
3. **Planning forums**. On-site, half-day meetings for upper management to review progress and adjust strategic plans.
4. **Staff meetings**. On-site, half-day updates for all employees on company progress and on general development topics.
5. **Communications meetings**. On-site, two-hour meetings on company status.
6. **New employee orientation**. A multiweek process involving meeting with other employees, reading materials, watching video tapes and following computer-aided training courses to obtain an understanding of the vision of the company and the general development required to be productive.
7. **Seminars**. Multiday, single-speaker presentations addressing specific development topics.

8. **Trade shows**. Multiday shows where specific development will result from interacting one-on-one with people having experiences relevant to company needs.

9. **Plant tours**. Visits to plants to obtain specific development on systems applications.

10. **Professional society meetings**. Meetings containing a brief presentation on general interest topics.

11. **Trade and professional journals**. A variety of publications addressing every manufacturing theme and aspect.

12. **Books**. Both general-interest and specific-interest books that provide in-depth coverage of a topic.

13. **Video tapes**. To illustrate and demonstrate the functions and application of equipment and systems.

14. **Equipment files**. Well-maintained files on vendor equipment and systems literature.

15. **Topic files**. Files containing articles, proceedings, and speeches on specific topics of interest.

16. **Client files**. Files containing proposals, reports, and supporting materials documenting past client interactions.

17. **Industry files**. Files containing clipped information on companies and industries which are marketing targets.

18. **Competition files.** Files containing literature and background information on all competition.

19. **Client data base**. A computerized data base of all past clients and all past equipment/systems applications. A referencing guide to direct users to the appropriate client files for information.

20. **Equipment cost guides**. A computerized guide to allow costing out of alternative equipment and systems.

21. **In-house development**. Specific development meetings where new software or technical methodologies are presented and illustrated.

22. **On-the-job development**. The utilization by a senior person of a real project to develop a less-experienced person on project technology and methodology.

TRUST

Hiring a winner and providing for the person's development is not enough to keep him motivated and happy. There must also be trust. You must realize that without trust:

1. There are no motivated and happy employees,
2. There is no respect, and thus, no loyalty,

3. There is no participation and no success, and

4. There is no winning manufacturing.

At IBM, this trust is manifested in the respect of the individual. At Delta Airlines, trust is called the family feeling, and at Hewlett-Packard, it is the HP way.

When trust exists, employees and managers have respect for each other. From respect comes a sincere desire to listen, which results in understanding the other's perspective. Understanding results in a concern for another's well-being; concern grows into a participative style that allows management and employees to openly discuss goals and directions. In turn, this leads to success, which gives way to positive reinforcement that makes employees happy and motivates them to work for further positive reinforcement. This is winning. The result is winning companies and employees. Management and employees establish a range of healthy communication that results in continuous winning. It all occurs because, up front, there was trust.

Without trust, companies have pursued a whole legacy of programs to attempt to obtain employee participation. There is absolutely nothing wrong with these programs. In fact, in companies where trust exists, these programs work very well. However, without trust, these concepts become fads about which the employees will moan and think this too shall pass. The issue is not which program is applied; the issue is one of basic trust. If there is no trust, there is no winning.

Some may take exception to my use of the term *employees* in this book. Some prefer to call employees partners, associates, stakeholders, or members. There is nothing wrong with these terms, but without trust, the terminology is of little importance. In fact, if there is trust, there is no problem with the term employees. All of the management books, the discussions on employee involvement and participation, and the fixation with Japanese success really boil down to achieving a mutual trust between management and employees. Only when every manager is dedicated to hiring, developing, and trusting winners will employees be motivated and happy. Only then will companies win.

HOW TO CREATE AN ENVIRONMENT WHERE EVERY EMPLOYEE IS MOTIVATED AND HAPPY

The creation of an environment where every employee is motivated and happy requires a long-term, consistent effort through winning manufacturing. The achievement of this requires:

1. A lasting commitment to winning manufacturing,
2. The confidence of all employees in the lasting commitment to winning manufacturing,
3. The development of all employees,
4. A mutual trust among all employees, and
5. The cooperation and teamwork of all employees.

There are no short cuts or easy solutions. Only by pursuing the process of winning manufacturing will an environment exist where every employee is motivated and happy and where winning manufacturing companies can be created.

REFERENCES

Brown, W.S. 1985. *13 Fatal Errors Managers Make and How You Can Avoid Them*. Fleming H. Revell Company. Old Tappan, New Jersey.

Gunn, T.G. 1987. *Manufacturing for Competitive Advantage: Becoming A World Class Manufacturer*. Ballinger Publishing Company. Cambridge, Massachusetts.

Haas, E.A. 1987. Breakthrough manufacturing. *Harvard Business Review*. March-April. Vol. 65, no. 2.

Hayes, R.H., and Wheelwright, S.C. 1984. *Restoring Our Competitive Edge: Competing Through Manufacturing*. John Wiley & Sons. New York.

Peters, T.J., and Waterman, R.H. 1982. *In Search of Excellence*. Harper and Row. New York.

Solomon, J. 1988. When are employees not employees? When they're associates, stakeholders.... *Wall Street Journal*. November 9.

Weiss, A. 1984. Simple truths of Japanese manufacturing. *Harvard Business Review*. July-August. Vol. 62, no. 4.

Chapter 18
TEAM PLAYERS

EVERYONE ASSOCIATED WITH MANUFACTURING MUST WORK TOGETHER AS A TEAM.

The concept of dynamic consistency requires everyone associated with manufacturing to have a consistent vision of manufacturing. Teamwork must exist—with your suppliers, within your organization, and with your customers—and will result in a desire for mutual success and cooperation. There is no winning manufacturing without it.

Manufacturing managers believe in teamwork, but unfortunately it has rarely been translated into action. Selfishness, machoism, and a belief that someone can only win when someone else loses has put the focus on one-upmanship, petty politics, and dishonesty in many organizations. Most experienced manufacturing people could fill a book describing vendors who were victimized, internal politics that lead to counterproductive activities, and customers who were not properly treated. These activities must be eliminated. Upper management must mandate and set an example that clearly indicates:

1. The enemy is the competition, not the vendors, the organization, or the customers.
2. The achievement of winning manufacturing requires the teamwork of all vendors, all internal functions, and all customers.
3. All adversarial relationships are unacceptable and must be eliminated.

TEAMWORK: SUPPLIERS AND CUSTOMERS

Follow the golden rule when establishing the supplier-customer relationship: treat your vendors like you want to be treated by your customers. When pursuing the golden rule, winning manufacturing companies will seek relationships based upon the following:

1. **Friendship**. The supplier and customer will establish a positive, mutually rewarding relationship. All levels of the organization will communicate frequently. There will be an open, honest flow of information between suppliers and customers. A genuine concern for the other's business will develop and suppliers and customers will become family.

2. **Limited sources**. Customers will deal with far fewer suppliers. Suppliers will have fewer, larger-volume customers. Suppliers will certify quality before it is shipped.

3. **Longterm relationships**. The supplier and customer will work together for the long term. All interactions will be done without any concern for the duration of the relationship as the relationship will be assumed to be never-ending.

4. **Quality**. Quality is defined in terms of customer requirements. Quality will be a joint concern and when problems occur, the supplier and the customer will work in unison to correct them. Requirements will be well-understood and will be consistently met.

5. **Integration**. Suppliers and vendors will be integrated via a common material tracking and control system. Suppliers will function like remote focused factories.

6. **Schedules**. The suppliers and customers will work together to establish a regular schedule for delivery. Customers will understand the importance of minimizing frequent changes in demand, and suppliers will understand the importance of meeting delivery schedules. Suppliers and customers will jointly believe in minimum-inventory, balanced, continuous-flow manufacturing.

7. **Joint improvement process**. The supplier and customer will be committed to helping each other. Suppliers and customers will have a dynamic, consistent vision of winning manufacturing.

TEAMWORK: WITHIN AN ORGANIZATION

A few illustrations of the importance of teamwork within an organization have already been covered: the importance of teamwork between manufacturing and marketing; and the product development benefits of having customers, marketing, product designers, process designers, purchasing, vendors, and manufacturing working as a team. Teamwork in other areas is equally important, and you should follow these guiding principals for creating teamwork:

1. All organizational units must be 100 percent directed toward the success of the total organization.
2. There will be no adversarial relationships within the organization.
3. All backbiting politics, one-upmanship, power plays, and so on will be eliminated.
4. All organizational units will function as a cohesive unit.

It is also important to address the teamwork among the layers within an organizational unit. (This aspect of teamwork was covered in Chapter 17.) An environment where every employee is motivated and happy will eliminate the we-they problem that destroys teamwork. In winning manufacturing, there are no we-they relationships; there are only team players.

HOW TO DEVELOP A WINNING MANUFACTURING TEAM

Basketball teams, Lions Club teams, and winning manufacturing teams are all developed by the following process:

1. Identify a leader.
2. Identify team players.
3. Specify the characteristics of a successful team.
4. Establish cooperation.
5. Establish a plan.
6. Obtain success.
7. Build upon the success. Return to Step 4.

The selection of the leader of a team is critical, as the team will ultimately reflect the leader's beliefs. The second step, identify team players, is an important prerequisite for the creation of a successful team. No amount of coaching, managing, or leading can create a team if the players are not committed to the task. An important question that must be asked early in the team building process is, "Do we have the right players?" The right players must meet three criteria:

1. Do the players really want to be a part of the team?
2. Do the players have the abilities that are required by the team?
3. Are the players truly committed to the success of the team?

The third team-building step is to specify the characteristics of a successful team. All team members must understand these characteristics, which will serve as the criteria for determining the team development. For winning manufacturing, the characteristics of a successful team are:

1. **Shared vision.** All team players will have a consistent vision of where the team is headed. Manufacturing teamwork will only exist when the vision of winning manufacturing is adopted by all team players.
2. **Shared values.** All winning manufacturing team players will adopt and adhere to a level of business ethics and honesty beyond levels that have been traditionally viewed as the norm. Team players will realize that a code of ethics is not a rules book on do's and don'ts, but is the moral fiber of the team players. High ethical standards may result in the loss of some short-term opportunities, but in the long run, they will provide a basis for teamwork and trust. All winning manufacturing team players will have unquestionable ethics.
3. **Shared expectations.** There will be no surprises for winning manufacturing team players. The team will have well-defined and understood expectations that are shared by all team players and serve as the basis for teamwork.
4. **Shared commitment.** There is no such thing as a part-time team player. Team players will be committed to the team and dedicated to the mutual success and cooperation of all team players.
5. **Shared confidence.** Each team player will have confidence in all other team players. Teamwork will be conducted with the anticipation of each team player performing his role. There will be no backbiting politics, adversarial relationships, or power plays.
6. **Shared responsibility.** Communications, involvement and interactions will be frequent. Team players will share responsibility for success and problems. Team players will be accountable for their efforts and for the team's performance.
7. **Shared rewards.** All team players will be rewarded for the team's performance. The team players will benefit from the team's success. Teamwork will be rewarded as the most important ingredient in winning manufacturing.

Establishing cooperation is the fourth step in creating a successful team. Cooperation cannot be created by having meetings or writing memos; it requires joint participation on a project. It takes time and will grow as the team succeeds. For winning manufacturing, it is critical to realize that sincere cooperation will not occur until after manufacturing improvements are implemented.

The fifth and sixth team building steps will result in the success needed to increase cooperation, which will increase the team's strength and its ability to make increasingly significant improvements.

The seventh step is the positive reinforcement of the team's success. For winning manufacturing, the seventh step is the end of one cycle of the winning manufacturing process (see Figure 1) and the beginning of the next cycle. Because of the success in implementing plans, the team increases its commitment, dedication, and therefore, its cooperation with the winning manufacturing team. This demonstrates the continuous improvement aspects of winning manufacturing and the evolutionary growth in the strength of the winning manufacturing team.

REFERENCES

Bennett, A., 1988. Ethics codes spread despite skepticism. *Wall Street Journal.* July 15.

Hayes, R.M., and Wheelwright, S.C. 1984. *Restoring Our Competitive Edge: Competing Through Manufacturing.* John Wiley & Sons. New York.

Melloan, G. 1988. Business ethics and the competitive urge. *Wall Street Journal.* August 9.

Peters, T. 1987. *Thriving on Chaos: Handbook for a Management Revolution.* Alfred A. Knopf. New York.

Schonberger, R.J. 1986. *World Class Manufacturing.* Free Press. New York.

Chapter 19
SIMPLIFICATION

ALL MANUFACTURING MUST BE SIMPLIFIED.

Complexity and simplicity are in the mind of the beholder. What is complex to one person can be simple to another. In your area of expertise, aren't there many things you know that are straightforward and intuitive to you, but beyond comprehension to others? The determination of an item's complexity or simplicity depends upon its inherent complexity and the understanding of the person making the determination. Simplification, therefore, involves reducing complexities and increasing understanding. Thus, the Requirement of Success that all manufacturing must be simplified means that manufacturing must be streamlined and better understood.

Winning manufacturing will streamline manufacturing in the following four areas:

1. Simplified product design,
2. Simplified manufacturing processes,
3. Simplified operating systems, and
4. Simplified organizational structure.

Streamlining will give all employees a broader, more accurate understanding of manufacturing. Thus, as the complexities are dissolved, the mysteries of manufacturing shall be uncovered and manufacturing will be simplified.

SIMPLIFIED PRODUCT DESIGN

It is interesting to note that the results of group technology, value analysis, failure mode and effect analysis, Taguchi methods, simultaneous engineering, design for manufacture, design for assembly, design for automation, and mechatronics are always the same:

design for simplicity. Simplified product design has two very consistent characteristics:

1. The reduction of the number of parts in a product, and
2. The use of standard parts.

As these two characteristics are achieved—
—manufacturing costs are reduced,
—production lead times are reduced,
—uncertainty is reduced,
—balance is easier to achieve,
—inventories are reduced,
—quality is increased,
—reliability is increased,
—maintenance is simplified,
—adaptability is increased,
—automation is easier to justify,
—material flow is simplified, and
—material tracking and control is simplified.

In brief, simplified product design is a facilitator of winning manufacturing. The reduction of the number of parts and use of standard parts are important characteristics of winning manufacturing that have a simplifying impact throughout manufacturing.

SIMPLIFIED MANUFACTURING PROCESSES AND OPERATING SYSTEMS

Traditional manufacturing is very complex. The production of complex products through non-focused departments that are overflowing with inventory is difficult to understand. Materials are released to the floor with an anticipation that, in several weeks, finished goods will result. The process of production is complex. The systems managing production are complex. No one person really understands how finished goods are produced. There simply is too much confusion, expediting, and uncertainty, and too many exceptions, changes, and deviations to comprehend the manufacturing processes or systems of traditional manufacturing.

To the contrary, in winning manufacturing, processes, and operating systems can be easily understood. Sufficient visibility exists not only to comprehend, but to literally watch products being produced. The winning manufacturing Requirements of Success leading to the simplified manufacturing process and the operating systems are:

1. Simplified product design,
2. Reduced lead times,
3. Reduced production lot sizes,
4. Reduced uncertainty,
5. Balanced, focused departments and factories,
6. Straightforward and transparent production and inventory control systems,
7. Reduced inventories,
8. Increased adaptability,
9. Increased quality,
10. Reduced down times,
11. Continuous-flow manufacturing, and
12. Upgraded material tracking and control systems.

Pursuing these Requirements of Success will simplify manufacturing processes and operating systems.

SIMPLIFIED ORGANIZATIONAL STRUCTURE

Complex organizational structures were created as attempts to control complex traditional manufacturing operations. Unfortunately, as organizational structures became more complex, organizations had an even greater problem in controlling manufacturing. As the problems increased, organizational structures grew in size and complexity. This, of course, led to even greater control problems which, in turn, led to further increases in organizational structures. This escalating spiral resulted in small spans of control, large corporate staffs and far too many organizational layers. Middle management proliferated. Because no one had enough control or comprehension of what really was happening, everyone spent their entire day in meetings. Rarely did anyone make decisions or take action; everyone just attended meetings. This frustrated upper management, so they created more staff positions and more layers of middle management to make something happen. Of course, what occurred was just the opposite. Now there were just more people to call or attend the meetings. The complexity got worse, manufacturing was out of control, and the meetings got larger and longer.

Complex organizational structures will not exist in winning manufacturing. Since winning manufacturing will be understandable, there will be people who truly understand manufacturing and they will be in control of their responsibilities. They will be able to make decisions and will be accountable for them. Because their positions will be controllable, they will be able to handle a much broader span of control. Since they will be able to make decisions, there will be a significantly reduced role for corporate staffs. Since there will be accountability, there will be significant reductions in the number of layers in an organizational structure.

A typical manufacturing organization chart for a winning manufacturing operation is given in Figure 29. There is no reason for any more than four layers in a winning manufacturing organization. Manufacturing will be simplified, and the organizational structure supporting manufacturing should be too.

HOW TO SIMPLIFY MANUFACTURING

Winning manufacturing is simplified manufacturing. As the process of winning manufacturing is pursued, simplified manufacturing— including product designs, manufacturing processes, and operating systems—will follow.

As winning manufacturing is implemented, the need for many layers of middle management will be eliminated, a task that needs to be done by upper management.

The approach that should be taken to eliminate the unneeded layers is:

1. As the process of winning manufacturing begins, the ultimate winning manufacturing organizational structure should be established.
2. The ultimate winning manufacturing organizational structure should be compared to the existing organizational structure. In all areas where more layers exist than should ultimately exist, a hiring freeze should be implemented.
3. As people leave the company, realignment should always be done in pursuit of the ultimate winning manufacturing organizational structure.
4. Depending upon the priorities established for pursuing winning manufacturing, a specific schedule for simplifying the organizational structure should be established and followed. For example, as focused factories are implemented, the ultimate materials management, engineering, financial and operations organizations should be implemented; as the integration of manufacturing and marketing takes place, the ultimate marketing and operations organizations should be implemented; as lead times are reduced or the global marketplace is addressed, the ultimate sales organization should be implemented; as product development is addressed, the ultimate research and development organization should be implemented, and so on.

Strict adherence to this approach is very important. Product design, manufacturing processes and operating systems simplifica-

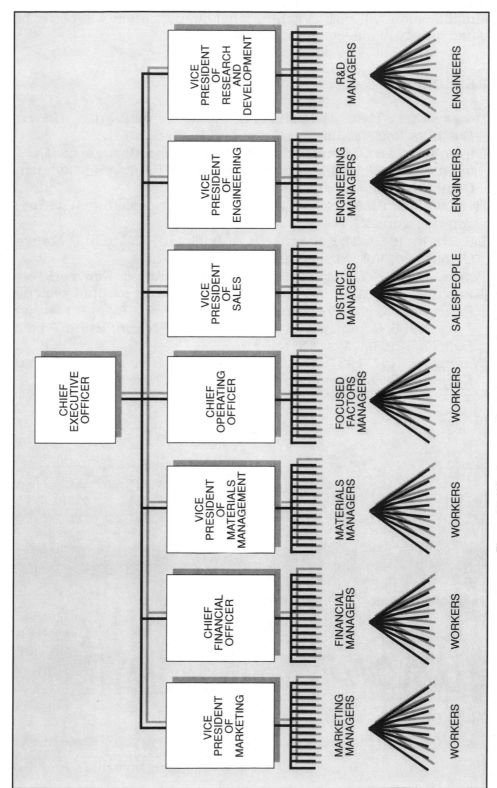

Figure 29. Winning manufacturing organization chart

155

tion will occur as winning manufacturing is pursued; organizational simplification will not. Organizational simplification will occur because upper management makes it happen.

REFERENCES

Drucker, P.F. 1988. The coming of the new organization. *Harvard Business Review*. January-February. Vol. 66, no. 1.

Gunn, T.G. 1987. *Manufacturing for Competitive Advantage: Becoming a World Class Manufacturer*. Ballinger Publishing Company. Cambridge, Massachusetts.

Hymowitz, C. 1988. A survival guide to the office meeting. *Wall Street Journal*. June 21.

Labick, K. 1988. The seven keys to business leadership. *Fortune*. October 24. Vol. 118, no. 9.

Peters, T. 1987. *Thriving On Chaos*. Alfred A Knopf. New York.

Tompkins, J.A. 1986. Automation: the secret of manual systems. *Industrial Product Bulletin*. August. Vol. 43, no. 7.

_____. 1986. Complexity: a sure path to disaster. *Industrial Product Bulletin*. August. Vol. 43, no. 7.

Waterman, R.H. 1987. *The Renewal Factor: How the Best Get and Keep the Competitive Edge*. Bantam Books. New York.

Chapter 20
INTEGRATION

ALL ORGANIZATIONS AND OPERATIONS MUST BE INTEGRATED.

Integration is the combining of elements to form a whole. The synergy that results from combining elements results in benefits that far exceed those that result from the summation of the elements. The integrated whole is truly more than the sum of its elements.

Figure 30 illustrates that several layers of integration go into winning manufacturing. Level 4 integration is winning manufacturing; it is the result of integrating the Level 3 elements of integrated organizations and operations.

PREREQUISITES OF WINNING MANUFACTURING INTEGRATION

The two prerequisites of winning manufacturing integration are dynamic consistency and interface standards. Unless you clearly understand these integration requirements, there will be no integration, and thus, no winning manufacturing.

Integration can only occur in the context of dynamic consistency. First, elements can only be integrated if they have a consistent mission. Secondly, integration can only survive when the elements that are being combined are allowed to be dynamic. Since organizations and operations are in constant change, long-lasting integration requires that adaptability is built into the integration process.

As an illustration of dynamic, consistent integration, consider an example of an automated guided vehicle system (AGVS) with a robot. For the AGVS to be integrated with the robot, a consistent mission including the dimensions, tolerances and weights of the parts,and the performance criteria must be established. For the integration to be long-lasting, a series of dynamic parameters need to be in place

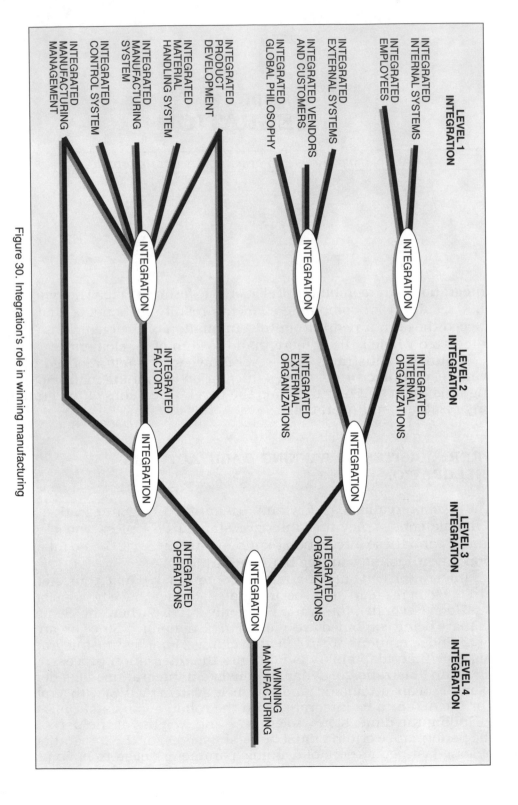

Figure 30. Integration's role in winning manufacturing

so that the range of future integration applications for the AGVS and the robot could be established.

The second integration prerequisite is the requirement of interface standards. Prior to attempting to integrate elements, standards must be established for the interface between elements. In the case of the AGVS and robot illustration, standards must be established for the positioning of parts for the physical interface to function. Standards must also be established for the communications between the AGVS control system and the robot control system in order for the communications interface to function. In general:

1. Material handling interface standards must be established to include unit load size, weight, and identification.
2. Communication interface standards must define the information protocol.

In addition to these standards, many more simple interfaces must be established. For example, it is important that:

1. Marketing, sales, and manufacturing establish a standard unit of measure so they may communicate without confusion. It is unacceptable for marketing to measure performance in square feet, sales in dollars, and manufacturing in pounds. A single, companywide unit of measure should be established.
2. Sales, production planning, and manufacturing establish a standard method for defining shipping performance. It is unacceptable for sales to measure performance based on the time from obtaining the order to customer receipt, for production planning to measure performance based on the time from release to the shop floor to customer receipt, and for manufacturing to measure performance based on the time from release to the shop floor to shipment.

LEVEL 3: INTEGRATED ORGANIZATIONS

As illustrated in Figure 30, integrated organizations are both internal and external. Internal ones result from the integration of the Level 1 elements' internal systems and employees. Similarly, external ones result from the integration of the Level 1 elements' external systems, vendors and customers, and global philosophy. These Level 1 integrated elements are:

1. Internal systems,
2. Personnel,
3. External systems,
4. Vendors and customers, and
5. Global philosophy.

Integrated Internal Systems

Figure 31 illustrates the concept of internal systems clouds, which are outgrowths of the traditional organizational responsibilities and the opposite of integration. The connecting lines represent a wide variety of interfaces via computer terminal, reports, memos, or telephone calls. As organizations grow, the organizational clouds become less responsive, efficient, and effective. Communication within the organization is slow and inaccurate. Many meetings are a direct result of the poor communication. The standard operating procedure is made up of chaos, uncertainty, and confusion. Organizational clouds are not a part of winning manufacturing.

Organizational clouds should be replaced by Computer Integrated Manufacturing (CIM), as illustrated by Figure 32. Unfortunately, several companies have made CIM an end unto itself, and this is counterproductive. The essence of CIM is that by using standard information protocols and an integrated corporate data base, communications within an organization will improve. With CIM, all organizational functions will be marching to the same drummer.

The computer aspects of CIM, such as communication networks, the utilization of mainframe computers, minicomputers, microcomputers, and programmable controllers or software development considerations, are technological issues that will continue to evolve. The important CIM issues that must be understood here are:

1. In winning manufacturing, a responsive adaptable, and reliable computer system must support CIM.
2. Winning manufacturing requires that all CIM information is quality information.
3. For a winning manufacturing company where all manufacturing will be simplified, where inventories will be reduced, where continuous flow, balance, and quality will be the norm, and where politics will be virtually eliminated, the planning, design, and implementation of CIM will be much more straightforward than for a traditional manufacturing company.
4. Winning manufacturing requires that CIM encompass an entire manufacturing company. It is because CIM has this broad scope that CIM must be designed from the top. Only after an overall CIM architecture is in place can the portions of CIM be successfully implemented.
5. In winning manufacturing, CIM will not be the integration of the computers. CIM will be the integration of the functions of manufacturing through the use of the computer.
6. In winning manufacturing, CIM will be viewed as a long-term, evolving strategy. CIM cannot be bought. CIM is not a software package. CIM is a continuing, ongoing program of advancement.

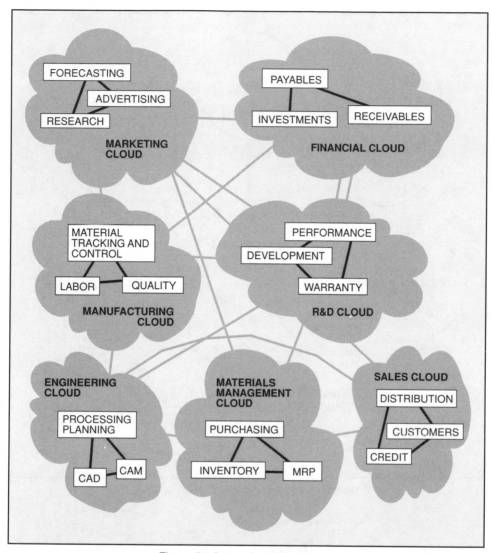

Figure 31. Internal systems clouds

7. In winning manufacturing, the CIM journey will be based upon a methodical plan. The CIM plan will undergo continuous change and update, but the overall CIM architecture will remain in place.

Integrated Employees

Winning manufacturing must have integrated employees. Organizations that implement CIM but who do not trust their employees and establish teamwork will not achieve winning manufacturing. The only way to establish integrated internal organizations is via the integration of CIM and integrated employees who are happy, motivated team players.

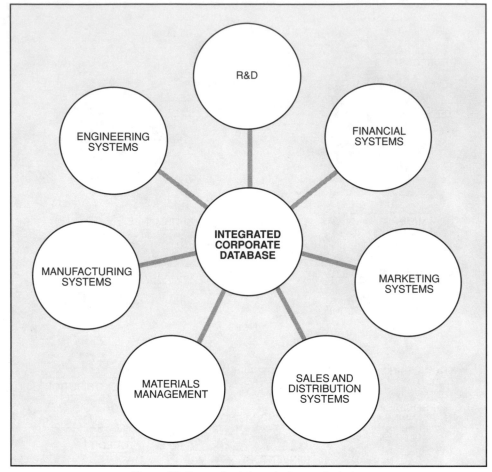

Figure 32. Computer integrated manufacturing

Integrated External Systems

Because the proper approach to integrate external systems is for the vendor and the customer to be integrated just as two focused factories in a plant are integrated, Figure 33 illustrates how integrated external systems can be tied in to the integrated internal system via electronic data interchange.

Integrated Vendors and Customers

The term used in this book for the integration of vendors and customers with winning manufacturers is teamwork. Once again, the guiding principal in establishing the proper vendor-customer-winning manufacturing relationship is the golden rule.

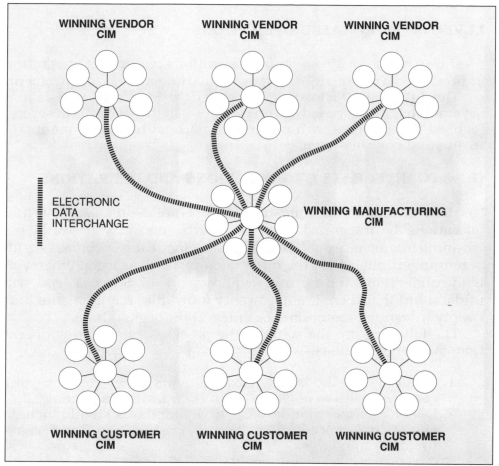

Figure 33. External–internal systems integration

Integrated Global Philosophy

The critical point that must be made here is that the participation in the global marketplace should not be done as a separate business. For the global marketplace to truly help a company amortize its product development costs over units sold around the globe, the global marketplace must be treated as an integrated portion of its domestic business. It is only by integrating the integrated global philosophy with integrated domestic operations that the synergistic benefits of addressing the global marketplace are realized. Thus, integrated global product development, integrated global manufacturing systems and integrated global logistics networks are important elements of winning manufacturing.

LEVEL 3: INTEGRATED OPERATIONS

As shown in Figure 30, integrated operations require the integration of product development, factory, and manufacturing management.

The integrated factory as illustrated in Figure 34 consists of several integrated focused factories. These, in turn, consist of several focused departments with integrated material handling, manufacturing and control systems.

HOW TO INTEGRATE ORGANIZATIONS AND OPERATIONS

If I had to answer the question "How should organizations and operations be integrated?" in two words, my answer would be, "winning manufacturing." Winning manufacturing encompasses all of manufacturing and is the integration of all its aspects. When you truly understand the twenty Requirements of Success, you will understand that there are not twenty individual requirements, but twenty integrated requirements. Integration begins there.

The following are the steps in the process of integrating operations and organizations.

1. Confirm that the twenty Requirements of Success are your company's vision of where your organization is heading.
2. Define interface standards. These standards should include operational, procedural, computer, organizational and measurement standards.
3. Pursue specific Requirements of Success while taking into consideration all twenty requirements and the interface standards.
4. Implement improvements for the specific Requirements of Success that were pursued.
5. Integrate improved operations with ongoing improved operations.
6. Repeat steps 3, 4 and 5. Continue to pursue improvements. Continue to pursue winning manufacturing.

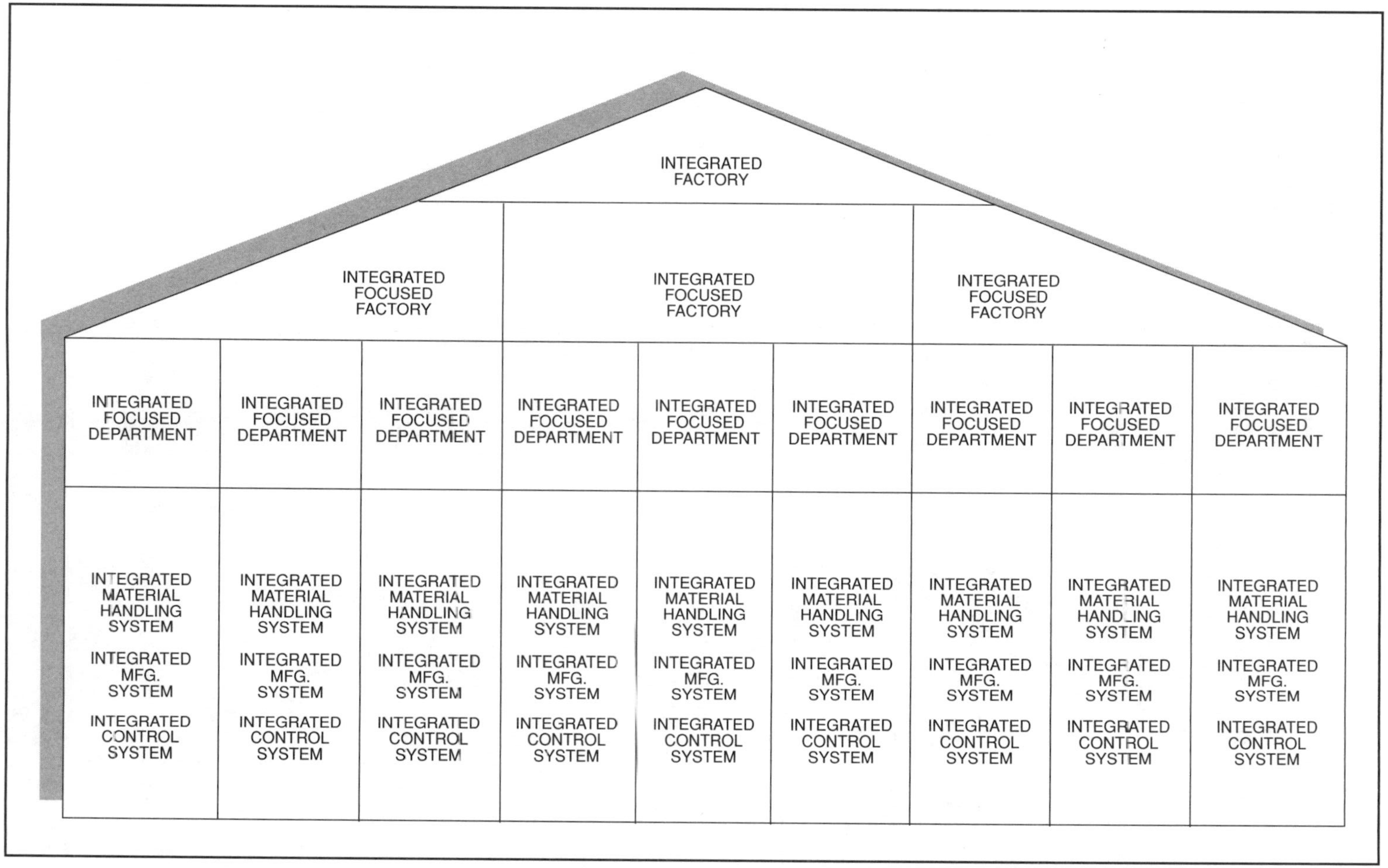

INTEGRATED FACTORY

INTEGRATED FOCUSED FACTORY

INTEGRATED FOCUSED DEPARTMENT

INTEGRATED MATERIAL HANDLING SYSTEM
INTEGRATED MFG. SYSTEM
INTEGRATED CONTROL SYSTEM

Figure 34. Integrated factory

REFERENCES

Calderwood, L. 1989. EDI: taking it from the top. *Materials Management and Distribution*. January. Vol. 34, no. 1.

Gunn, T.G. 1987. *Manufacturing for Competitive Advantage: Becoming a World Class Manufacturer*. Ballinger Publishing Company. Cambridge, Massachusetts.

Harrington, J.J. 1978. *Computer Integrated Manufacturing*. Krieger Publishing Company. Huntington, New York.

Martin, J.M. 1988. CIM: what the future holds. *Manufacturing Engineering*. January. Vol. 100, no. 1.

Tompkins, J.A. 1986. CIM is great: but what do you do? *Modern Materials Handling*. August. Vol. 41, no. 9.

_____. 1987. Giving CIM a chance. *Modern Materials Handling*. May. Vol. 42, no. 6.

_____. 1987. The scope and thrust of CIM. *Modern Materials Handling*. April. Vol. 42, no. 5.

_____. 1986. The truth about islands of automation. *Modern Materials Handling*. December. Vol. 41, no. 15.

_____. 1984. Successful facilities planner must fulfill role of integrator in the automated environment. *Industrial Engineering*. May.

Wallach, S.L. 1988. For users of CIM, the plan's the thing. *Managing Automation*. July. Vol. 3, No. 7.

Chapter 21
UNDERSTANDING

MANUFACTURING MANAGEMENT MUST UNDERSTAND WINNING MANUFACTURING.

Winning requires an understanding of the sport, particularly in team sports where each team player must understand the fundamentals of the game, the strategy for scoring, and the roles of the team players.

Winning manufacturing is much like a team sport. It requires that manufacturing management understand the fundamentals of winning manufacturing, the strategies for winning manufacturing, and the roles of team players.

Integrated manufacturing management is a team that has a full, consistent understanding of these fundamentals, strategies, and roles.

UNDERSTANDING THE FUNDAMENTALS FOR WINNING MANUFACTURING

Manufacturing managers must understand the two fundamentals of winning manufacturing.

1. A prerequisite of winning manufacturing is a commitment to winning.
2. A prerequisite of winning manufacturing is technical intimacy.

If manufacturing management is not committed to winning, winning manufacturing is not obtainable. Manufacturing management must reject:

1. Fads, gimmicks and quick fixes,
2. Fire-fighting and short-term optimization,
3. Incremental analysis, and
4. Petty politics and adversarial relations.

Manufacturing management must be dedicated to the long-term pursuit of winning manufacturing and to the reality that there is no easy answer. Hard work, dedication, persistence, teamwork, and clear, consistent decision making are the only ways to achieve winning manufacturing.

An outgrowth of the commitment to winning is the need for an in-depth, intimate understanding of the technical aspects of manufacturing. In other words, manufacturing management must understand manufacturing.

Starting in the late 1960s, a group of American managers came to believe excellence in management is transferrable; that is, if I can manage a bank, I can manage a factory or a hospital. This group did not believe that management had to concern itself with the technical aspects of a company because, after all, management is management.

A 1974 *Harvard Business Review* article claimed that three types of skills are needed to be an effective manager:

1. **Technical skill**. Specialized knowledge and ability to perform specific types of activities, for example, how a machine operates.
2. **Human skill.** The ability to work as a team member and leader.
3. **Conceptual skill.** The ability to see the enterprise as a whole and understand its interrelatedness.

The article explained that technical skills are important to lower levels of management, but unimportant to upper-level management. Human skills are important to all management levels, but conceptual skills are important only to upper management.

The article was wrong. Upper management must have the technical skills and the technical intimacy to understand manufacturing. Lower levels of management must have the conceptual skills to understand how their decisions impact the whole of manufacturing. A fundamental of winning manufacturing is that all levels of management must have strong technical, human, and conceptual skills. Otherwise, a manager will not be able to ask the right questions, evaluate the answers, or make the right decisions.

Technical intimacy requires both intellectual understanding and first-hand experience, and the only way to obtain the first-hand experience is out on the shop floor. Thus, all levels of manufacturing management must spend time on the shop floor.

UNDERSTANDING THE STRATEGY FOR WINNING MANUFACTURING

The strategy for winning manufacturing is the dynamic, consistent vision of winning manufacturing presented throughout this book. By understanding the twenty Requirements of Success as the formula for winning manufacturing, the manager understands the strategy for achieving winning manufacturing.

UNDERSTANDING THE ROLES OF TEAM PLAYERS

Team players have two roles: team leader or team member. Team leaders are not managers, because winning manufacturing cannot be achieved by management that organizes, plans, directs, measures, and controls. Winning manufacturing team leaders establish the vision of where the firm is headed, select good people, clearly delegate, coordinate, and get out of the way. The winning manufacturing team leader is a pacesetter, a facilitator, and a motivator. The winning manufacturing team leader will:

1. Be certain everyone has a shared vision of winning manufacturing;
2. Make sure everyone has a clear understanding of their responsibilities;
3. Create an environment where people want to participate;
4. Make certain that the right people are doing the right jobs;
5. Be visible in support and setting an example, but invisible in decision making, except where needed, and in obtaining recognition;
6. Assure that the right people receive proper recognition;
7. Understand that each person has a different motivation, perspective, and objective, and that each must be guided and encouraged differently;
8. Have wide-angle vision and understanding of the big picture of where an operation is headed;
9. Have the ability to look beyond the problems of the present operations and focus on the opportunities of the future;
10. Through enthusiasm, create excitement and urgency among the team members;
11. Be an excellent listener;
12. Not procrastinate;
13. Be driven by a desire for continuous improvement;
14. Be interested in obtaining an adequate return on investment, as well as in doing what will ensure the firm's success; and
15. Be certain that all decisions are made by the appropriate level in the organization.

All employees of a manufacturing company pursuing winning manufacturing should be team members, who are the company's experts on the specific tasks they perform. No one knows their tasks better, thus, no one is better able to improve them, and no one is better qualified to make decisions about their tasks. The responsibilities of the team members are to:

1. Adopt the shared vision of winning manufacturing,
2. Understand how their tasks are affected by the shared vision of winning manufacturing,
3. Continuously improve their tasks within the context of the shared vision of winning manufacturing,
4. Work with other team members to improve the integration of tasks,
5. Participate with other team members and leaders for the improvement of the company,
6. Communicate with leaders on opportunities for improvement,
7. Be accountable for the implementation of improvements,
8. Accept full ownership of improvements,
9. Accept full responsibility for decisions best made by them, and
10. Be an enthusiastic team player.

HOW TO FACILITATE MANUFACTURING MANAGEMENT'S UNDERSTANDING OF WINNING MANUFACTURING

A word of caution is appropriate here: some managers cannot be made to understand winning manufacturing. These managers are stubbornly set in their ways. They do not disagree with winning manufacturing; they simply are not interested in change. They cannot be helped, and they will not help your pursuit of winning manufacturing.

When faced with a resistant manager, you have four choices:

1. Work around the resistant manager.
2. Eliminate the resistant manager.
3. Assume the resistant manager's responsibilities.
4. Leave the company.

Although these choices may seem severe, they are the only ones. I have spent, and I have seen others spend, inordinate amounts of time trying to convert resistant managers. It cannot be done.

Most manufacturing managers will be skeptical about winning manufacturing. This is healthy and, in fact, preferred. Manufacturing managers who too easily desire to pursue winning manufacturing may be viewing winning manufacturing as the next quick fix.

The process of understanding must begin with an awareness of winning manufacturing. A winning manufacturing pioneer should be identified to carry out the task. The pioneer does not have to be the chairman of the winning manufacturing program; the pioneer's job is to coordinate manufacturing management's understanding of winning manufacturing.

If you are not properly positioned to be your company's pioneer, then your next step should be to identify who is. You should contact this person, lend them this book, and encourage them to read it.

If you are properly positioned to be your company's winning manufacturing pioneer, the steps you should follow to make manufacturing management aware of winning manufacturing are:

1. Study this book. Be sure you understand winning manufacturing.
2. Do a preliminary prioritization of the Requirements of Success.
3. Send a memo similar to the memo given in Figure 35 to your manufacturing leadership.
4. Conduct a one-hour winning manufacturing review meeting (see Appendix A for the details of this meeting). The objective of the winning manufacturing review meeting is to motivate manufacturing management to read this book. Distribute the book to the manufacturing leadership and schedule a winning manufacturing commitment meeting.

TO: MANUFACTURING LEADERSHIP

FR: WINNING MANUFACTURER PIONEER

RE: WINNING MANUFACTURING

     I HAVE RECENTLY READ A BOOK THAT, IN A VERY STRAIGHTFORWARD MANNER, EXPLAINED WINNING MANUFACTURING. THE BOOK TOUCHES ON MANY OF THE THINGS WE HAVE BEEN DOING TO IMPROVE MANUFACTURING. HOWEVER, THE BOOK'S COMPLETENESS AND COMMON SENSE APPROACH HAVE CONVINCED ME THAT WE CAN BENEFIT BY PURSUING THE ISSUE FURTHER.

     SPECIFICALLY, I BELIEVE THAT BY ESTABLISHING A PROGRAM OF WINNING MANUFACTURING, WE CAN MAKE SIGNIFICANT PROGRESS IN:

1. **LIST THE REQUIREMENTS**
2. **OF SUCCESS THAT YOU**
3. **IDENTIFIED AS THE**
4. **HIGHEST PRIORITIES.**

     I RECOMMEND THAT AS A FIRST STEP WE HAVE A ONE-HOUR MEETING TO REVIEW THE CONCEPT OF WINNING MANUFACTURING. I WILL CHAIR THIS SESSION.

     THE MEETING WILL TAKE PLACE AT_____ ON _____ IN CONFERENCE ROOM_____. I LOOK FORWARD TO YOUR ATTENDANCE.

Figure 35. Winning manufacturing introductory memo

After the meeting, manufacturing management will be aware of winning manufacturing. To obtain manufacturing management's commitment to winning manufacturing, a winning manufacturing commitment meeting must be held (see Appendix B) to achieve the following objectives:

1. Be certain your manufacturing management understands the Requirements of Success.
2. Obtain a commitment to pursue winning manufacturing.
3. Appoint a winning manufacturing chairman.
4. Establish a date for the initiation of the winning manufacturing visionary development process.

The chairman will function as the champion, coordinator, and facilitator of winning manufacturing. This person should be an experienced manufacturing manager whose sole responsibility is winning manufacturing.

When the winning manufacturing commitment meeting is over, the pioneer's work is done. Manufacturing management understands winning manufacturing and has a winning manufacturing chairman. The chairman's task is presented in Chapter 22.

REFERENCES

Fechter, W., and Horowitz, R.B. 1988. The role of the industrial supervisor in the 1910s. *Industrial Management.* May-June.

Hayes, R.H., and Wheelwright, S.C. 1984. *Restoring our Competitive Edge: Competing Through Manufacturing.* John Wiley & Sons. New York.

Katz, R.L. 1974. Skills of an effective administrator. *Harvard Business Review.* September-October. Vol. 52, no. 5.

Peters, T. 1987. *Thriving on Chaos: Handbook for a Management Revolution.* Alfred A. Knopf. New York.

Peters, T.J., and Austin, J. 1985. *A Passion for Excellence.* Random House. New York.

Peters, T.J., and Waterman, R.H. 1982. *In Search of Excellence.* Harper and Row. New York.

Pfeiffer, W.J. 1986. *Strategic Planning: Selected Reading.* University Associates, Inc. San Diego, California.

Prentice, W.C.H. 1961. Understanding leadership. *Harvard Business Review.* September-October. Vol. 39, no. 5.

Tompkins, J.A. 1987. CIM champions. *Modern Materials Handling.* February.

_____. 1986. NEA: the answer to manufacturing automation

excellence. *Industrial Product Bulletin*. January. Vol. 43, no. 1.

_____. 1987. Project management vs. project leadership. *Industrial Product Bulletin*. February. Vol. 44, no. 2.

Waterman, R.H. 1986. *World Class Manufacturing*. Free Press. New York.

Wortman, D. 1986. CIM and simulation. *Manufacturing Systems*. April. Vol. 6, no. 4.

Zaleznik, A. 1989. Real work. *Harvard Business Review*. January-February. Vol. 67, no. 1.

Chapter 22
A CALL TO ACTION

GO MAKE SOMETHING HAPPEN.

Winning manufacturing is a never-ending journey toward continuous improvement. Your company's success in achieving winning manufacturing depends upon your company's desire to move forward and its ability to get started. What is required now is action.

The method of pursuing winning manufacturing is:

Phase I: Winning Manufacturing Awareness
Phase II: Winning Manufacturing Commitment
Phase III: Winning Manufacturing Visionary Develoment
Phase IV: Winning Manufacturing Planning
Phase V: Winning Manufacturing Execution

Table 15 presents the actions and references for each phase (see Appendix E).

I have titled this concluding chapter "A Call To Action" because I want to emphasize how important I believe it is for you to act. I believe your company needs winning manufacturing to survive. I believe this book has presented a program for you to pursue winning manufacturing. It is all worthless, however, unless you take action. You *do* make a difference. Your active participation in winning manufacturing will make a difference. The next step is action. Go, Make Something Happen!

Appendix A
Winning Manufacturing
Review Meeting

I. OBJECTIVE: To motivate manufacturing management to read
                            this book

II. MEETING LEADER: Winning manufacturing pioneer

III. MEETING PREPARATION: None

IV. PARTICIPANTS: Manufacturing management

V. DURATION: One hour

VI. AGENDA: A. Dynamic consistency
                            B. Winning manufacturing
                            C. Overview of Requirements of Success
                            D. Method of pursuing winning manufacturing
                            E. Overview of *Winning Manufacturing*
                            F. Assign readings of *Winning Manufacturing*
                            G. Schedule winning manufacturing commitment
                            meeting

VII. MEETING HANDOUT: Winning Manufacturing Review Meeting
                            Month, Day, Year
                            Conference Room____

I. *Winning Manufacturing* by Dr. James A. Tompkins, President of Tompkins Associates, Inc.

II. Three types of organizations
        Type I: Static Consistency
        Type II: Dynamic Inconsistency
        Type III: Dynamic Consistency

III. **Winning manufacturing.** A process of continuous manufacturing improvement based upon a long-term commitment to a broad-based, common-
sense, structured approach.

IV. **Requirements of success**. The consistent direction for manufacturing and the basis for continuous improvement.
- — Manufacturing costs
- — Manufacturing and marketing
- — Product development
- — Global marketplace
- — Lead times
- — Production lot sizes
- — Uncertainty
- — Balance
- — Production and inventory control
- — Inventories
- — Adaptability
- — Quality
- — Maintenance
- — Material flow
- — Material tracking and control
- — Human resources
- — Team players
- — Simplification
- — Integration
- — Understanding

V. Method of pursuing winning manufacturing
Phase I: Winning Manufacturing Awareness
Phase II: Winning Manufacturing Commitment
Phase III: Winning Manufacturing Visionary Development
Phase IV: Winning Manufacturing Planning
Phase V: Winning Manufacturing Execution

VI. *Winning Manufacturing*
- 22 chapters plus appendices
- Chapter 1: Overview
- Chapters 2-21: Twenty Requirements of Success and how-tos
- Chapter 22 and appendices: The method of pursuing winning manufacturing

VII. Action Items
- Read *Winning Manufacturing*
- Winning manufacturing commitment meeting
Date:
Time:
Location:

Appendix B
Winning Manufacturing
Commitment Meeting

I. OBJECTIVES:

1. To be certain manufacturing management understands the Requirements of Success
2. To obtain a commitment to pursue winning manufacturing
3. To appoint a winning manufacturing chairman
4. To establish a date for the initiation of the manufacturing visionary development process

II. MEETING LEADER:

Winning manufacturing pioneer

III. MEETING PREPARATION:

All meeting participants should read *Winning Manufacturing*

IV. PARTICIPANTS:

Same as for the Winning Manufacturing Review Meeting

V. DURATION:

Two or three hours

VI. AGENDA:

A. Review meeting objectives
B. Review Requirements of Success
C. Review method of pursuing winning manufacturing
D. Appoint winning manufacturing chairman
E. Establish schedule

VII. MEETING HANDOUT:

Winning Manufacturing Commitment Meeting
Month, Day, Year
Conference Room ____

I. Meeting Objectives
— Understand Requirements of Success
— Commit to winning manufacturing
— Appoint winning manufacturing chairman
— Establish schedule for winning manufacturing visionary development process

II. Requirements of Success
A. **Manufacturing costs**. Manufacturing costs must be significantly reduced.

    - Improve, improve, improve
    - Significant cost reductions
    - Today's manufacturing costs
    ____% direct labor
    ____% material costs
    ____% overhead costs

B. **Manufacturing and Marketing.** Manufacturing and marketing must become integrated and function as a team.
    - Today's relationship
    - Customization, customer expectations, and forecasts
    - Opportunity for synergism

C. **Product Development**. Product development must become an integrated, iterative process.
    - Today's approach
    - Today's market responsiveness
    - Opportunity for integrated, iterative process

D. **Global Marketplace.** All manufacturing decisions must be made within the context of an integrated global strategy.
    - Today's global impact
    - Product development
    - Manufacturing
    - Global logistics

E. **Lead Times**. Significant reductions in lead times must occur.
    - Today's lead times
    - Customer requirements for lead times
    - Opportunities for lead time reductions

F. **Production Lot Sizes**. Production lot sizes and setup times must be reduced.
    - Today's lot sizes
    - Today's setup times
    - Opportunities for lot size and setup time reductions

G. **Uncertainty.** All uncertainty must be minimized, discipline must be increased.
    - Today's level of certainty
    - Status of standards
    - Status of discipline

H. **Balance**. All manufacturing operations must be balanced.
    - Focused departments
    - Continuous flow
    - Sequential flow
    - Standardization

I. **Production and Inventory Control**. The production and inventory control system must be straightforward and transparent.
    - Present status
    - Impacts of winning manufacturing
    - Opportunities for improvement

J. **Inventories**. Drastic reductions in inventories must occur.
    - Today's inventory levels
    - Impacts of winning manufacturing
    - Opportunities for inventory reduction

K. **Adaptability**. Manufacturing facilities, operations, and personnel must become more adaptable.
    - Flexibility and modularity
    - Current status
    - Opportunities for increases in adaptability

L. **Quality**. Product quality, vendor quality, and information quality must improve.

    - Today's approach to quality
    - Understanding customer requirements
    - Quality control and quality assurance
    - Information quality
    - Opportunity for improving quality

M. **Maintenance**. Manufacturing process failures must be minimized.
    - Who does maintenance today
    - Present commitment to maintenance
    - Opportunity for improving

N. **Material Flow**. Material flow must be efficient.
    - Status of present material flow
    - Continuous-flow manufacturing
    - Opportunity to increase efficiency of material flow

O. **Material tracking and control**. Material tracking and control systems must be upgraded.
    - Response time
    - Use of automatic identification and electronic data interchange
    - Opportunity for upgrade

P. **Human Resources**. Every manager must be dedicated to creating an environment where every employee is motivated and happy.
    - Present approach to development
    - What is current level of trust
    - Opportunity to improve employee satisfaction

Q. **Team players**. Everyone associated with manufacturing must work together as a team.
    - Supplier and customer relations
    - Internal teamwork
    - Opportunity for improved relationships

R. **Simplification**. All manufacturing must be simplified.
    - Simplified product design
    - Simplified manufacturing processes
    - Simplified operating systems
    - Simplified organization structure

S. **Integration**. All organizations and operations must be integrated.
    - Status of material handling standards
    - Status of communication standards
    - Status of computer integrated manufacturing (CIM)
    - Status of integrated operations

T. **Understanding**. Manufacturing management must understand winning manufacturing.
    - Fundamentals, strategy, and rules
    - Method of pursuing winning manufacturing
    - Needs for improvement

III. Method of pursuing winning manufacturing
    Phase I: Winning Manufacturing Awareness
    Phase II: Winning Manufacturing Commitment
    Phase III: Winning Manufacturing Visionary Development
    Phase IV: Winning Manufacturing Planning
    Phase V: Winning Manufacturing Execution

IV. Winning manufacturing at _____ (your company)
    A. Commitment

B. Winning manufacturing chairman
C. Winning manufacturing visionary development schedule

Appendix C
Winning Manufacturing Prioritization Meeting

I. OBJECTIVE:

To reach a consensus on which five to seven Requirements of Success should be the focus for the next winning manufacturing improvement cycle

II. MEETING LEADER:

Winning manufacturing chairman

III. MEETING PREPARATION:

All meeting participants should complete and return a manufacturing manager's priorities questionnaire (Figure 2). The winning manufacturing chairman should summarize the participants' inputs and establish a recommended list of prioritized Requirements of Success.

IV. PARTICIPANTS:

Same as for the winning manufacturing review and commitment meetings

V. DURATION:

One hour

VI. AGENDA:

A. Review summary of the responses to the manufacturing manager's priorities questionnaire
B. Recommended prioritized Requirements of Success
C. Open discussion
D. Establish a consensus on the prioritized Requirements of Success for the next winning manufacturing improvement cycle

VII. MEETING HANDOUT:

Winning Manufacturing Prioritization Meeting
Month, Day, Year
Conference Room_____

I. Meeting objective: To reach a consensus on the prioritized Requirements of Success for the next winning manufacturing improvement cycle.

II. Summary of manufacturing managers' priorities questionnaires (total number of responses___)

III. Recommended prioritized Requirements for Success for the next winning manufacturing improvement cycle.

REQUIREMENTS OF SUCCESS	TOTAL POINTS	AVERAGE POINTS	PRIORITY
A. MANUFACTURING COSTS			
B. MANUFACTURING AND MARKETING			
C. PRODUCT DEVELOPMENT			
D. GLOBAL MARKETPLACE			
E. LEAD TIMES			
F. PRODUCTION LOT SIZES			
G. UNCERTAINTY			
H. BALANCE			
I. PRODUCTION AND INVENTORY CONTROL			
J. INVENTORIES			
K. ADAPTABILITY			
L. QUALITY			
M. MAINTENANCE			
N. MATERIAL FLOW			
O. MATERIAL TRACKING AND CONTROL			
P. HUMAN RESOURCES			
Q. TEAM PLAYERS			
R. SIMPLIFICATION			
S. INTEGRATION			
T. UNDERSTANDING			

REQUIREMENTS OF SUCCESS	GOAL
A. MANUFACTURING COSTS	
B. MANUFACTURING AND MARKETING	
C. PRODUCT DEVELOPMENT	
D. GLOBAL MARKETPLACE	
E. LEAD TIMES	

Figure 36 (Part 1). Sample questionnaire for rating and goal setting

REQUIREMENTS OF SUCCESS	GOAL
F. PRODUCTION LOT SIZES	
G. UNCERTAINTY	
H. BALANCE	
I. PRODUCTION AND INVENTORY CONTROL	
J. INVENTORIES	
K. ADAPTABILITY	
L. QUALITY	
M. MAINTENANCE	
N. MATERIAL FLOW	
O. MATERIAL TRACKING AND CONTROL	
P. HUMAN RESOURCES	
Q. TEAM PLAYERS	
R. SIMPLIFICATION	
S. INTEGRATION	
T. UNDERSTANDING	

Figure 36 (Part 2). Sample questionnaire for rating and goal setting

PRIORITY	REQUIREMENT OF SUCCESS
1	
2	
3	
4	
5	
6	
7	

Figure 37. Sample priority chart

Appendix D
Winning Manufacturing Requirements Of Success Initiation Meetings

---

I. OBJECTIVE:

A series of meetings will be required, one for each prioritized Requirement of Success. The objective of each meeting shall be to obtain the organization's commitment and understanding of each of the prioritized Requirements of Success.

II. MEETING LEADER:

Winning manufacturing chairman

III. MEETING PREPARATION:

All people attending the meeting should have attended the winning manufacturing orientation briefing (see Appendix E).

IV. PARTICIPANTS:

The strongest advocates from the winning manufacturing prioritization meeting for the specific Requirements of Success and the employees most affected by each requirement.

V. DURATION:

One hour

VI. AGENDA:

A. Review method of pursuing winning manufacturing
B. Present prioritized Requirements of Success
C. Present the goals that were discussed at the winning manufacturing prioritization meeting
D. Discuss the specific prioritized Requirements of Success
E. Open discussion
F. Present the action plan

VII. MEETING HANDOUT:

Winning Manufacturing Requirement of Success Initiation Meeting
Month, Day, Year
Conference Room _____

I. Method of pursuing winning manufacturing.
      Phase I: Winning Manufacturing Awareness
      Phase II: Winning Manufacturing Commitment
      Phase III: Winning Manufacturing Visionary Development
      Phase IV: Winning Manufacturing Planning
      Phase V: Winning Manufacturing Execution

II. Prioritized Requirements of Success
  A.
  B.
  C.
  D.
  E.
  F.
  G.

III. Conceptual prioritized Requirements of Success goals
  A.
  B.
  C.
  D.
  E.
  F.
  G.

IV. Understanding _____ (insert the prioritized Requirement of Success title). Include here the material for the prioritized Requirement of Success from the winning manufacturing management seminar (Appendix E).

V. _____ (insert the prioritized Requirement of Success title) action plan.

Action IVd:	Establish team (date)
Action Va:	Assess present status and identify specific goals (date)
Action Vb:	Identify and evaluate alternative approaches (date)
Action Vc:	Define and obtain support for improvement plans (date)
Action Vd:	Implement plans and audit results (date)

Winning Manufacturing Visionary Development

Visionary development is the understanding by all employees of the vision of winning manufacturing that results in shared beliefs, winning employees, and winning manufacturing companies.

Visionary development will result from the following four approaches:

Approach 1: Attend Winning Manufacturing Orientation Briefing
Approach 2: Read *Winning Manufacturing*
Approach 3: Attend Winning Manufacturing Management Seminar
Approach 4: Participate in Winning Manufacturing Study Groups

All employees should be assigned to one of the following five visionary development groups:

Group I: Upper Management
Group II: Middle Management and Engineers
Group III: Shop Floor Leadership
Group IV: Shop Floor Personnel
Group V: Administrative Personnel

Table 15 presents the visionary development approaches that should be used for each employee group. The remainder of this appendix describes visionary development Approaches 1, 3, and 4.

APPROACH 1

WINNING MANUFACTURING ORIENTATION BRIEFING

I. OBJECTIVE: To introduce the process of winning manufacturing to all employees

II. BRIEFING LEADER: Winning manufacturing chairman

III. MEETING PREPARATION: None

IV. PARTICIPANTS: All employees

V. DURATION: One hour

VI. AGENDA: A. Winning manufacturing
                           B. Dynamic consistency

TABLE 15
Visionary Development For Employee Groups

PHASE		ACTION	REFERENCES
I. Winning Manufacturing Awareness	IA: IB: IC: ID:	Identify the winning manufacturing pioneer The pioneer should study this book and fully understand winning manufacturing Conduct a winning manufacturing review meeting Manufacturing management should read *Winning Manufacturing*	Chapter 21 Chapters 1-22 Appendix A Chapters 1-22
II. Winning Manufacturing Commitment	IIA: IIB: IIC: IID:	Conduct a winning manufacturing commitment meeting Obtain manufacturing management's commitment to winning manufacturing Appoint a winning manufacturing chairman Establish a date for the initiation of the winning manufacturing visionary development process	Appendix B Chapters 1 and 21 Chapters 1 and 21 Appendix E
III. Winning Manufacturing Visionary Development	IIIA: IIIB: IIIC: IIID:	Assign all employees to a visionary development group Conduct a winning manufacturing orientation briefing Conduct a winning manufacturing management seminar Initiate winning manufacturing study groups	Appendix E and Chapter 7 Appendix E-Approach I Approach 3 Appendix E-Approach 4
IV. Winning Manufacturing Planning	IVA: IVB: IVC: IVD:	Distribute, collect and summarize the Manufacturing Management Priorities Questionnaire Conduct a winning manufacturing prioritization meeting Conduct a winning manufacturing Requirement of Success initiation meeting for each prioritized Requirement of Success Establish a team for each prioritized Requirement of Success	Chapter 1-Appendix C Appendix C Appendix D Chapters 1 and 18
V. Winning Manufacturing Execution	VA: VB: VC: VD:	Assess present status and identify specific goals Identify and evaluate alternative approaches Define and obtain support for improvement plans Implement plans and audit results	Chapters 1-21 Chapters 1-21 Chapters 1-21 Chapters 1-21

C. Method of pursuing winning manufacturing
D. Commitment
E. Overview of Requirements of Success
F. Action plan

VII. BRIEFING HANDOUT: Winning Manufacturing Orientation Briefing
Month, Day, Year
Conference Room_____

 I. *Winning Manufacturing*
  A. *Winning Manufacturing* by Dr. James A. Tompkins, president of Tompkins Associates, Inc.
  B. A long-term commitment to a broad-based, common sense, structured process of continuous improvement

 II. Dynamic Consistency
  A. Type I Organizations: Static Consistency
  B. Type II Organizations: Dynamic Inconsistency
  C. Type III Organizations: Dynamic Consistency

 III. Method of Pursuing Winning Manufacturing
  A. Phase I: Winning Manufacturing Awareness
  B. Phase II: Winning Manufacturing Commitment
  C. Phase III: Winning Manufacturing Visionary Development
  D. Phase IV: Winning Manufacturing Planning
  E. Phase V: Winning Manufacturing Execution

 IV. Commitment
  A. On (date) our CEO (name) made a commitment

to winning manufacturing

B. (CEO name) has appointed (name) the winning manufacturing chairman

V. Requirements of Success

A. **Manufacturing costs**. Manufacturing costs must be significantly reduced.

B. **Manufacturing and marketing**. Manufacturing and marketing must become integrated and function as a team.

C. **Product development**. Product development must become an integrated, iterative process.

D. **Global marketplace**. All manufacturing decisions must be made within the context of an integrated global strategy.

E. **Lead times**. Significant reductions in lead times must occur.

F. **Production lot sizes**. Production lot sizes and setup times must be reduced.

G. **Uncertainty.** All uncertainty must be minimized, discipline must be increased.

H. **Balance**. All manufacturing operations must be balanced.

I. **Production and inventory control.** The production and inventory control system must be straightforward and transparent.

J. **Inventories.** Drastic reductions in inventory must occur.

K. **Adaptability**. Manufacturing facilities, operations, and personnel must become more adaptable.

L. **Quality**. Product quality, vendor quality, and information quality must improve.

M. **Maintenance**. Manufacturing process failures must be minimized.

N. **Material flow**. Material flow must be efficient.

O. **Material tracking and control**. Material tracking and control systems must be upgraded.

P. **Human resources**. Every manager must be dedicated to creating an environment where every employee is motivated and happy.

Q. **Team player**. Everyone associated with manufacturing must work together as a team.

R. **Simplification**. All of manufacturing must be simplified.

S. **Integration.** All organizations and operations must be integrated.

T. **Understanding**. Manufacturing management must understand winning manufacturing.

APPROACH 3
WINNING MANUFACTURING MANAGEMENT SEMINAR

I. OBJECTIVE: To provide a detailed understanding of the process of winning manufacturing, the method of pursuing winning manufacturing, and the Requirements of Success

II. SEMINAR LEADER: Winning manufacturing chairman

III. MEETING PREPARATION: All participants should have attended the winning manufacturing orientation briefing and read *Winning Manufacturing*

IV. PARTICIPANTS: Middle management and engineers (Group II), and shop floor leadership (Group III)

V. DURATION: One day

VI. AGENDA: A. Winning manufacturing
B. The twenty Requirements of Success
C. A call to action

VII. SEMINAR HANDOUT: Winning Manufacturing Management Seminar
Month, Day, Year
Conference Room_____

    I. Winning Manufacturing (Chapter 1)

A. Winning manufacturing is the process of continuous improvement.

B. Winning manufacturing must be based upon a consistent direction of where manufacturing is headed.

C. Traditional manufacturing has not done a good job of presenting a consistent direction.

D. Dynamic Consistency

    1. Type I Organizations: Static Consistency

    2. Type II Organizations: Dynamic Inconsistency

    3. Type III Organizations: Dynamic Consistency

E. Requirements of Success

    1. **Manufacturing costs**. Manufacturing costs must be significantly reduced.

    2. **Manufacturing and marketing.** Manufacturing and marketing must become integrated and function as a team.

    3. **Product development**. Product development must become an integrated, iterative process.

    4. **Global marketplace**. All manufacturing decisions must be made within the context of an integrated global strategy.

    5. **Lead times**. Significant reductions in lead times must occur.

    6. **Production lot sizes**. Production lot sizes and setup times must be reduced.

    7. **Uncertainty**. All uncertainty must be minimized; discipline must be increased.

    8. **Balance**. All manufacturing operations must be balanced.

    9. **Production and inventory control.** The production and inventory control system must be straightforward and transparent.

    10. **Inventories**. Drastic reductions in inventory must occur.

    11. **Adaptability**. Manufacturing facilities, operations and personnel must become more adaptable.

    12. **Quality**. Product quality, vendor quality, and information quality must improve.

    13. **Maintenance**. Manufacturing process failures must be minimized.

    14. **Material flow**. Material flow must be efficient.

    15. **Material tracking and control**. Material tracking and control systems must be upgraded.

    16. **Human resources**. Every manager must be dedicated to creating an environment where every employee is moti-

vated and happy.

17. **Team player**. Everyone associated with manufacturing must work together as a team.

18. **Simplification**. All of manufacturing must be simplified.

19. **Integration**. All organizations and operations must be integrated.

20. **Understanding**. Manufacturing management must understand winning manufacturing.

F. The process of winning manufacturing is given in Figure 38.

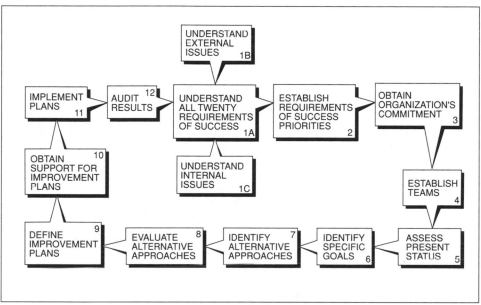

Figure 38. Winning manufacturing process

G. The process of winning manufacturing is continuous.

H. The process of winning manufacturing is based upon an integrated understanding of all twenty Requirements of Success.

I. The method of pursuing winning manufacturing
    1. Phase I: Winning Manufacturing Awareness
    2. Phase II: Winning Manufacturing Commitment
    3. Phase III: Winning Manufacturing Visionary Development
    4. Phase IV: Winning Manufacturing Planning
    5. Phase V: Winning Manufacturing Execution

II. **Manufacturing Costs**. Manufacturing costs must be significantly reduced (Chapter 2).
    A. Approaches to manufacturing cost reduction

        1. Type I Organizations: Static Consistency
        2. Type II Organizations:Dynamic Inconsistency
        3. Type III Organizations:Dynamic Consistency

B. Significant manufacturing cost reductions are cost reductions in the 40% to 60% range.

C. Today's manufacturing costs.
        1. Direct labor: 5% to 15%
        2. Material costs: 35% to 55%
        3. Overhead costs: 35% to 55%

D. The amount of effort allocated to manufacturing cost reduction should be proportional to the costs of manufacturing.

E. How to significantly reduce the costs of manufacturing
        1. Document present costs
        2. Define cost reduction goals
        3. Consider alternatives to reach goals
        4. Economically and qualitatively analyze alternatives
        5. Establish an improvement plan
        6. Sell the improvement plan to management
        7. Implement the improvement plan
        8. Audit implemented performance, and when necessary, take corrective action

III. **Manufacturing and marketing**. Manufacturing and marketing must become integrated and function as a team (Chapter 3).

A. Winning manufacturing cannot be achieved at the expense of another team player.

B. Ceasefire
        1. A truce mandated by upper management
        2. Establish mutual understanding

C. Peace
        1. Requires communications and a long-term commitment to unison
        2. Higher levels of customization will be demanded by your customers
        3. Marketing must define the customer's true desires and needs to manufacturing
        4. Manufacturing and marketing must understand the role and impact of forecasts

D. Synergism
        1. Manufacturing and marketing become integrated
        2. Figure 39 illustrates manufacturing and marketing synergism

E. How to integrate manufacturing and marketing to function as a team
        1. Ceasefire
        2. Peace
        3. Synergy

IV. **Product development**. Product development must become an integrated, iterative process (Chapter 4).

A. Product development is the interactive process whereby the customer, marketing, sales, product designers, process designers, purchasing, vendors, and manufacturing work together to develop a product that meets customers' expectations and may be economically manufactured.

B. Traditional product development: throw it over the wall.

C. The evolution of winning manufacturing product development is given in Figure 40.

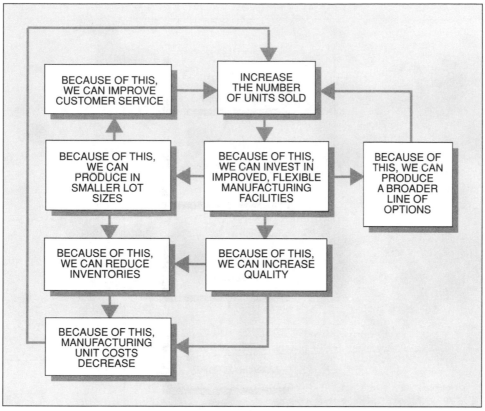

Figure 39. Synergistic benefit of winning manufacturing on an integrated manufacturing-marketing team

D. Figure 41 illustrates the time span from product conception to product availability for both traditional and winning manufacturing product development

E. Winning manufacturing product development is preferred because a better, lower-cost product is brought to market sooner

F. Product development issues

    1. Team players

    2. Simplification

    3. Integration

    4. Understanding

G. How to establish an integrated, iterative product development process

    1. Establish a product team

    2. Define product team task

    3. Document product assumptions, customer needs, customer wants, product restrictions, and manufacturing requirements

    4. Establish specific product goals

    5. Establish product development priorities

    6. Pursue the product development process given in Figure 42

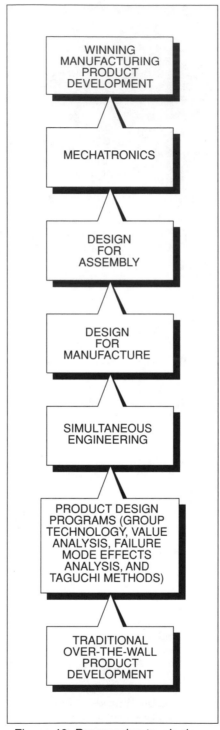

Figure 40. Progression to winning
manufacturing product
development

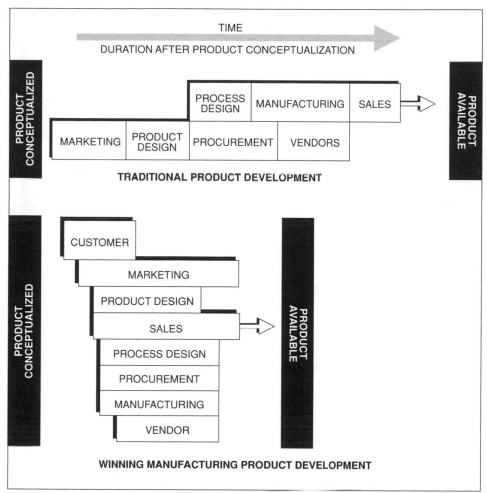

Figure 41. Duration from product conceptualization to product availability

V. **Global marketplace**. All manufacturing decisions must be made within the context of an integrated global strategy (Chapter 5).

   A. The significant increase in the involvement in the global marketplace will be even greater in the future

   B. The motivating force to be involved in the global marketplace is survival

   C. Why must companies be global?

      1. Higher product development costs

      2. Technology increasingly has an important role in product development

      3. Product lives are shorter

      4. Because of these three points, higher product development costs must be amortized over a shorter product life

      5. The only acceptable method of amortizing the higher development costs over a short time period is by increasing the number of units sold

      6. However, with the shorter product life the only alterna-

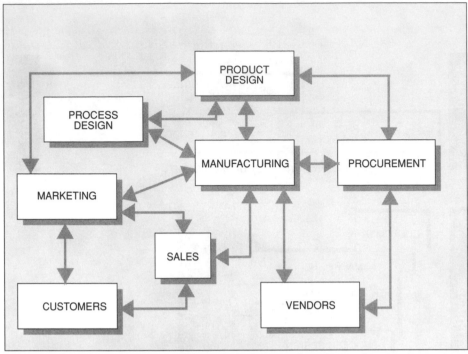

Figure 42. The functional interactions of winning manufacturing product development

tive to selling more units is to expand your marketplace; that is, to enter the global marketplace

D. Product development must be done while considering the global marketplace

E. A global product is one that has been developed while considering the needs for global customization, and because of its standardized platform, can be manufactured by standardized, flexible manufacturing systems for consumption in the global marketplace

F. Global manufacturing can be viewed from the perspective of offshore global manufacturing and global networks

    1. Care must be exhibited when considering producing products offshore, as burden most often remains in the domestic operation

    2. A winning manufacturing global network is no more than a network of winning manufacturing operations

G. Global logistics are no different from domestic logistics, just more complex

H. How to establish an integrated global strategy

    1. Assess your present global outreach

    2. Establish global goals

    3. Define a variety of approaches to achieve these goals

    4. Evaluate alternative approaches

    5. Identify best global strategy

    6. Sell management on the best global strategy

    7. Implement the global strategy

    8. Audit implementation

    9. Establish global strategy oversight group

VI. **Lead times**. Significant reductions in lead times must occur (Chapter 6).
  A. Definitions
    1. **Manufacturing lead time.** The time from material availability at the first manufacturing operation until the last manufacturing operation is complete
    2. **Production lead time**. The time from the ordering of all materials for an items production, until the last manufacturing operation is complete
    3. **Customer lead time**. The time between customer ordering and customer receipt
  B. Lead times are what management decides they should be
  C. Winning manufacturing knows
    1. Long lead times make it impossible to plan and control priorities
    2. Shorter lead times clear the shop floor of work-in-process inventory, conflicting manufacturing priorities, and manufacturing problems
    3. The only controllable lead times are short lead times
  D. Reducing lead time results in
    1. Reduced inventories
    2. Quicker response to customers
    3. Improved employee satisfaction
    4. Improved quality
    5. Reduced costs of manufacturing
  E. The obtainable reduction in lead time depends upon the historical approach to lead time and the amount of product customization
    1. The less attention that has historically been focused on lead time, the greater is the opportunity for lead time reduction
    2. The less customization in a product, the greater the opportunity for lead time reduction
  F. How to significantly reduce lead times
    1. Document present customer lead times
    2. Competitive analysis
    3. Leadership must establish a goal
    4. Identify bottlenecks
    5. Create teams to pursue simplification, teamwork, and uncertainty

VII. **Production lot sizes.** Production lot sizes and setup times must be reduced (Chapter 7).
  A. As production lot sizes are reduced, so too will be the queue time, and thus, the manufacturing lead time
  B. As the number of operations increases, the greater the effect the production lot size has on manufacturing lead time
  C. The only way to maintain manufacturing efficiency while reducing production lot sizes is to reduce setup times
  D. Economic lot sizes
    1. The traditional approach to economic lot sizes says that the lot size that is most economical is the lot size where the setup cost equals the inventory carrying cost
    2. Given that
        S = Setup cost
        A = Annual usage
        Q = Economic lot size
        I = Cost of carrying inventory

C = Unit cost of an item in inventory
then:

$$Q = \sqrt{\frac{2AS}{IC}}$$

TABLE 16
The Effect Of Production Lot Size On Manufacturing Lead Times
(Processing 100 units through one-minute operations)

NUMBER OF OPERATIONS	MANUFACTURING LEAD TIME FOR LOT SIZE OF TWO (IN MINUTES)	MANUFACTURING LEAD TIME FOR LOT SIZE OF EIGHT (IN MINUTES)	PERCENT INCREASE IN MANUFACTURING LEAD TIME FOR AN IN-CREASE IN LOT SIZE FROM TWO TO EIGHT
2	102	108	6%
3	104	116	12%
4	106	124	17%
5	108	132	22%
6	110	140	27%
7	112	148	32%
8	114	156	37%

E. Toyota Motor Company setup time reduction
1. Concepts
a. Separate the internal setup from the external setup
b. Convert as much of the internal setup as possible to external setup
c. Eliminate the adjustment process
d. Abolish the setup
2. Techniques
a. Standardize the external setup actions
b. Standardize the machines
c. Use quick fasteners
d. Use a supplementary tool
e. Consider multiperson setup crews
f. Automate the setup process
F. How to reduce production lot sizes
1. Document present lot sizes
2. Identify setup times
3. Reduce setup times
4. Calculate economic lot size
5. Identify alternative methods for handling the economic lot size between operations
6. Evaluate alternatives for efficient material handling
7. Justify the investment required to reduce setup times and to efficiently handle materials with the savings resulting from the reduction in lot size
8. Define and obtain support for specific improvement plans

9. Implement the reduced setup time and the material handling equipment as justified; begin production of reduced lot sizes.

VIII. **Uncertainty**. All uncertainty must be minimized; discipline must be increased (Chapter 8).
    A. Everything that happens will happen according to plan
    B. In winning manufacturing there is insufficient time to deal with unplanned and untimely events
    C. All activities must have well-established, clear standards, and all activities must conform to these standards
    D. The traditional fire-fighting manufacturing manager who specializes in managing uncertainty will be replaced by a winning manufacturing manager who specializes in managing certainty
    E. Once standards are established, discipline must be applied to achieve conformance; there are to be no exceptions
    F. How to minimize uncertainty (Figure 43)

IX. **Balance.** All manufacturing operations must be balanced (Chapter 9).
    A. More important than the speed of any operations will be the balance of a series of operations
    B. The starting point in achieving balance is determining the cycle time that must be met to satisfy production requirements
    C. Focused department
        1. A focused department results when all the operations required to produce a family of parts are located in a focused area
        2. Focused department facilitates balance
    D. Focused factories
        1. Provide for the balance and support of a series of focused departments
        2. Consist of focused receiving departments, shipping, material handling, and management
    E. Continuous flow
        1. Balancing a series of operations having small lot sizes requires continuous, controlled indexing of parts through production
        2. WIP inventory buffers may be required when continuous flow is not possible; these WIP inventory buffers should not be long-term storage locations, but mere hesitations in the continuous flow of material
    F. Sequential flow is a requirement of absolute balance; if it cannot be achieved, a WIP inventory buffer should be installed
    G. Standardization
        1. To achieve balance, all operations must be performed with certainty, according to a standard
        2. The Toyota Motor Company method for establishing a standard operation
            a. Determine the cycle time
            b. Determine elemental time
            c. Determine the standard operations routine
            d. Determine the standard quantity of WIP
            e. Document the standard of performance
    H. Balance must be understood in the context of the costs of manufacturing
        1. As the cost of a component increases, the most economical order cycle gets shorter

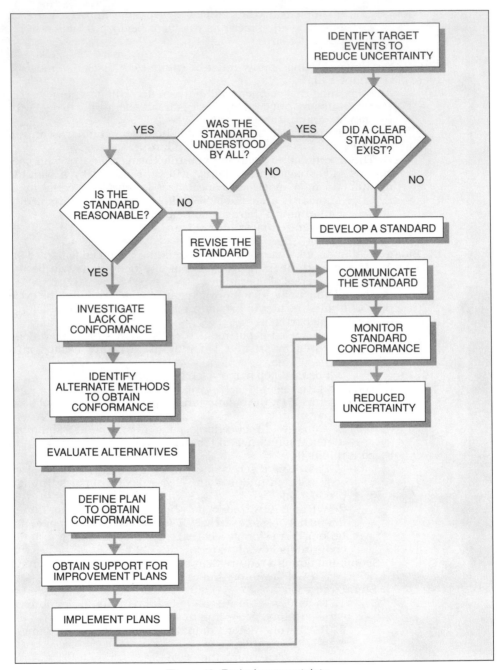

Figure 43. Reducing uncertainty

2. As the demand of a component increases, the most
economical order cycle gets shorter
I. WIP inventory buffers in front of a capacity bottleneck are often
justifiable; the size of the inventory buffer depends upon
1. The cost of the bottleneck equipment
2. The cost of the WIP inventory

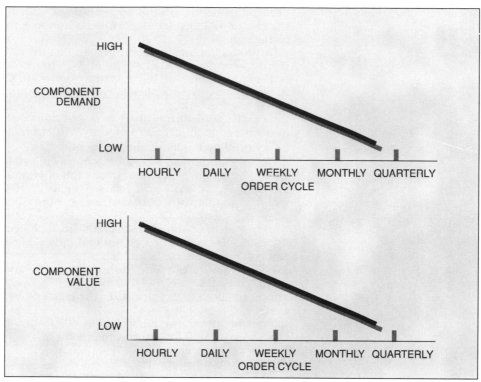

Figure 44. The relationship between order cycle and component demand and order cycle
and component value

3. The severity of the capacity bottleneck
J. The approach to the bottleneck capacity should be
    1. Use simulation to establish the proper level of WIP inventory buffer in front of the bottleneck operations
    2. Evaluate the cost of the WIP inventory buffer versus the cost of obtaining more capacity, and thus, eliminating the bottleneck; if the bottleneck is eliminated by the addition of more capacity, work towards achieving balance.
    3. If the bottleneck is not eliminated
        a. Maximize the speed of the bottleneck operations
        b. Balance nonbottleneck operations to maintain the proper WIP inventory buffer in front of the bottleneck operation
K. How to achieve balanced manufacturing
    1. Document present WIP inventory
    2. Identify opportunities by asking the following questions
        a. Have setup time reductions been implemented? What is the potential for setup time reductions? (Chapter 7)
        b. Have production lot sizes been reduced? What is the potential for production lot size reductions? (Chapter 7)
        c. Has uncertainty been minimized? What potential exists for minimization of uncertainty? (Chapter 8)
        d. Have focused departments and focused factories

been implemented? What opportunities exist for the creation of focused departments and focused factories?

e. Do production lot sizes continuously flow through manufacturing operations? Are all WIP inventory buffers justifiable? are WIP inventory buffers high-turnover, low-inventory hesitations in the continuous flow of materials?

f. Have the proper procedures been put in place to maximize sequential flow? How may WIP inventory be reduced by implementing sequential flow?

g. Have standards of performance been established, accepted, and followed for each operation, focused department, and focused factory? How may the standards of performance be more rigorously pursued?

h. Have the operational costs of just-in-time been analyzed? Is there a proper understanding of the tradeoff operating costs and balance?

i. Have capacity bottlenecks been properly analyzed? Has the issue of balance been properly addressed both before and after the capacity bottleneck?

j. If not already answered, why does WIP inventory exist? Are all WIP inventories justified?

3. Prioritize the opportunities
4. Identify and evaluate alternatives
5. Define, obtain approval, and implement improvement plans

X. **Production and inventory control**. The production and inventory control system must be straightforward and transparent (Chapter 10).

A. Production and inventory control systems in traditional manufacturing have been a major problem

B. The keys to a winning manufacturing production and inventory control system are

1. The production and inventory control system should be implemented as a portion of the winning manufacturing process

2. The production and inventory control system should be straightforward and transparent

3. The production and inventory control system should be MRP II-based

C. Production and inventory control in a winning manufacturing company will be radically different than production and inventory control in a traditional company

1. Manufacturing and marketing
2. Product development
3. Lead times and production lot sizes
4. Uncertainty and balance

D. Straightforward production and inventory control systems are systems that are easily understood

E. Transparent production and inventory control systems are systems that are logical and follow intuition

F. The steps that must be taken to control production and inventory

1. Define the product, families and options to be produced
2. Define the volume of products, families and options to be produced

3. Specify a production plan
4. Define when materials and capacity should be present to meet the production plan
5. Schedule material delivery from vendors
6. Schedule focused factories
7. Monitor schedule adherence
G. MRP II (Figure 45)

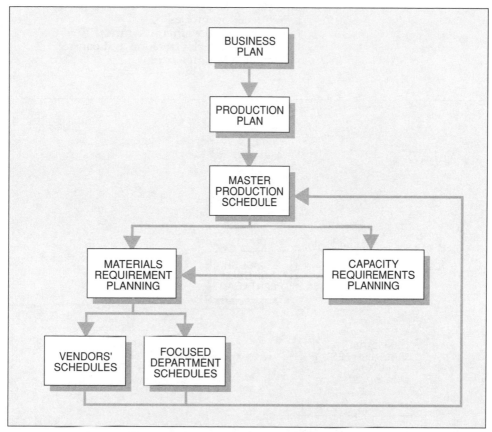

Figure 45. Manufacturing resource planning

H. The Toyota production and inventory control methodology (Figure 46)
I. The only difference between MRP II and the Toyota production and inventory control methodology is the method of generating the master production schedule
    1. With MRP II the master production schedule is based upon upcoming demand
    2. The Toyota production and inventory control system assumes a uniform rate of production
J. Winning manufacturing companies will use MRP II
K. How to establish a straightforward and transparent production and inventory control system
    1. Successful MRP II users should simplify their MRP II system

2. For companies not successful with MRP II, the approach should be
    a. Manufacturing and marketing synergy
    b. Simplified product design
    c. Reduced lead times
    d. Reduced production lot sizes
    e. Reduced uncertainty
    f. Balanced focused departments and focused factories
    g. Reduced inventories
    h. Continuous-flow manufacturing
    i. Improved material tracking and control
    j. Simplified MRP II system

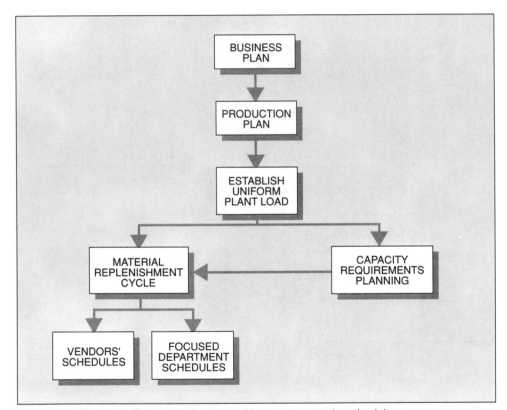

Figure 46. Toyota production and inventory control methodology

XI. **Inventories**. Drastic reductions in inventories must occur (Chapter 11).
    A. Inventory is expensive because of
        1. Cost of carrying inventory
        2. Manufacturing problems that are not addressed because the problems are obscured by inventory
    B. To reduce inventories, the problems that were the cause of the inventories must be removed; for example
        1. Finished goods inventories may be reduced and customer service improved by significantly reducing lead times
        2. Work-in-progress inventories may be reduced and manu-

facturing efficiency increased by significantly reducing setup times

3. Raw material inventories may be reduced and quantity discounts still achieved by working with vendors as team players

C. Eliminating problems that lead to the creation of inventory
    1. Manufacturing and marketing
    2. Product development
    3. Lead time
    4. Production lot sizes
    5. Uncertainty
    6. Balance
    7. Production and inventory control

D. Eliminating inventories will make it easier to maintain little or no inventory

E. How not to reduce inventories
    1. On the vendor's back
    2. The shell game
    3. Management mandate
    4. Hire more expediters
    5. Over-management

F. How to reduce inventories
    1. Document the present level of inventory
    2. Compare inventory levels to available yardsticks
    3. Establish an inventory reduction goal
    4. Perform an audit to determine why the present levels of inventory exists
    5. Identify specific approaches to reduce inventories
    6. Evaluate alternative approaches
    7. Integrate beneficial inventory reduction approaches
    8. Obtain support for the plan
    9. Implement the plan
    10. Audit results

XII. **Adaptability**. Manufacturing facilities, operations and personnel must become more adaptable (Chapter 12)

A. Adaptability has been a basic component of all prior Requirements of Success
    1. Adaptability is required for continuous improvement (Chapter 2)
    2. Adaptability is required to respond to inaccurate forecasts (Chapter 3)
    3. Adaptability is required to handle the increased pace of product development
    4. Adaptability is required to meet the customization necessary to be a global manufacturer (Chapter 5)
    5. Adaptability is required to provide quality customer service while maintaining low inventories (Chapters 6 through 11)

B. Definitions of adaptable
    1. The ability to become suitable for a new use
    2. The ability to produce different manufacturing requirements
    3. Flexibility and modularity
        a. Flexibility. The ability to handle a variety of requirements without being altered
        b. Modularity. The ability to expand or contract without altering the approach

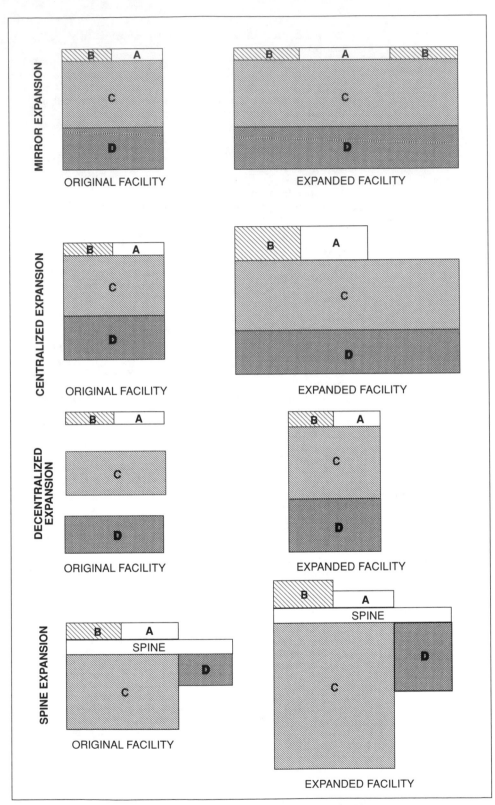

Figure 47. Block layouts for modular facilities

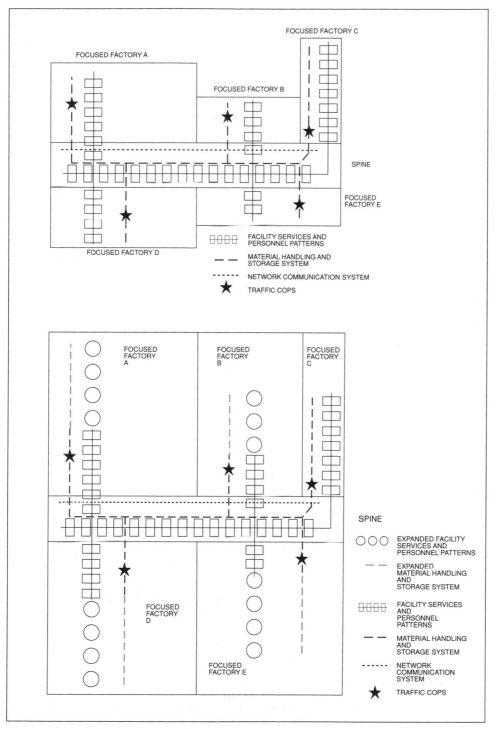

Figure 48. Illustration of a spine facility

c. Flexibility
    i. Focused factories (Chapter 9)
    ii. Small production lot sizes (Chapter 7)
    iii. Versatile equipment. Equipment should be selected with sufficient versatility to handle today's manufacturing requirements and when justifiable, future requirements.
        - Adjustable length, width, and depth equipment
        - Variable speed, rate and volume equipment
        - Future computer hardware and software
    iv. Multiskilled employees. Provide for improved speed, efficiency and quality.
    Approach
        - Production supervisors rotating through each job
        - Rotation of all personnel through each job
        - Scheduling multiskilled employees through all jobs

d. Modularity
    i. Modular facilities
        - Common approaches to facility expansion
        - Spine facilities
    ii. Modular focused departments. Establish modular job assignments to avoid trapping workers within inefficient work confines
    iii. Time modularity. Be creative with employee work schedules

e. How to achieve manufacturing adaptability
    i. Assess the adaptability of present plans, designs and ongoing operations; identify artificial barriers to flexibility and modularity
    ii. Identify flexibility and modularity requirements; establish specific goals for each of these requirements
    iii. Identify alternative approaches to achieving the specific flexibility and modularity goals
    iv. Evaluate the alternative approaches
    v. Specify the approaches that will best achieve the flexibility and modularity goals; define an improvement plan for achieving these goals
    vi. Obtain support for the improvement plan
    vii. Implement the plan
    viii. Audit results and further identify artificial barriers to flexibility and modularity

XIII. **Quality**. Product quality, vendor quality, and information quality must improve (Chapter 13).
    A. Quality has become a crusade
    B. It is time for less crusading, less hype and more understanding of quality
    C. Japan defines quality as satisfying the customer
    D. United States defines quality as conformance to requirements
    E. Quality is the conformance to customer requirements

F. Elements of quality for which a customer's requirements should be recorded
    1. Performance
    2. Features
    3. Reliability
    4. Conformance
    5. Durability
    6. Serviceability
    7. Aesthetics
    8. Perceived quality

G. Quality control is the design of the product and processes so that the conformance of the product to customer requirement is achieved
    1. Quality cannot be inspected into a product
    2. Quality cannot be built into a product
    3. Quality can only be designed into a product and the processes that produce the product

H. Quality assurance is the ongoing activity that ensures products conform to customer requirements

I. Total quality control is the combination of quality control and quality assurance

J. Evolution of quality
    1. Traditionally quality has been an operational, reactive activity
    2. Today quality control and quality assurance are proactive
    3. Today statistical process control is used to bring and maintain processes in control
    4. Quality will continue to progress; in winning manufacturing companies, quality will be
        a. Top-down driven from an awareness and commitment perspective
        b. Bottom-up driven from a measurement and reporting perspective
        c. Customer-driven from a requirements perspective
    5. Inspection will be done on all units, in-line on a real-time basis
    6. Inspection will be the hub of
        a. The control of the manufacturing process
        b. The reduction of variability and product tolerances; that is, increased consistency
        c. Feedback and machine calibration
        d. Real-time line stoppage and the identification of the reason for stoppage
        e. Predictive maintenance
        f. Management reporting
        g. Customer quality documentation
        h. Feedback to product and process planning

K. Information quality
    1. Quality information makes companies function
    2. The definition of quality information is accurate data organized in accordance with the requirements of the user
    3. Quality information
        a. Can be processed at very high speeds
        b. Is reusable
        c. Costs less now than ever before
        d. Can be made available to many sources virtually

simultaneously with the initial input
L. How to improve product, vendor and information quality
    1. Overview
        a. Quality is not free
        b. A successful quality improvement program should be a broad-based, participative effort involving an entire organization
        c. Before pursuing quality, a strong upper-management commitment to quality must be made
        d. This commitment must be broadly communicated
    2. Process
        a. Know your customer
        b. Define customer requirements
        c. Assess present quality performance
        d. Identify problems
        e. Specify alternative solutions
        f. Evaluate alternative solutions
        g. Establish improvement plans
        h. Implement improvement plans
        i. Audit results

XIV. **Maintenance**. Manufacturing process failures must be minimized (Chapter 14).
    A. In many manufacturing organizations, the function of maintenance does not get proper respect
    B. Traditional manufacturing companies have
        1. Under-emphasized preventive, corrective, and routine maintenance
        2. Not addressed predictive maintenance
        3. Not properly trained maintenance personnel
        4. Not properly developed maintenance management
        5. Because of these four items, excessive, unpredictable manufacturing process failures have resulted
    C. Without effective maintenance, machines and system will fail, and when failure occurs
        1. Certainty will not be achieved (Chapter 8)
        2. Balance will not be obtained (Chapter 9)
        3. Inventories will be required (Chapter 10)
    D. Levels of manufacturing maintenance
        1. Level I: Breakdown maintenance
        2. Level II: Routine maintenance
        3. Level III: Corrective maintenance
        4. Level IV: Preventive maintenance
        5. Level V: Predictive maintenance
    E. To support operator ownership, operators should perform Levels V, IV, III and as much Level II maintenance as is practical
    F. Winning manufacturing maintenance
        1. Reliability
        2. Redundancy
        3. Modularity
        4. Obsolescence
        5. Maintenance personnel
        6. Maintenance training and education
        7. Expert systems
        8. Working environment
        9. Maintenance management

10. Maintenance database
11. Maintenance storeroom
12. Maintenance inventory
13. Maintenance and engineering
14. Maintenance professionals

G. How to minimize manufacturing process failure
    1. Phase I: Management commitment to maintenance
        a. Educate upper management on the importance of maintenance to winning manufacturing
        b. Obtain upper management's commitment to effective manufacturing maintenance
        c. Communicate upper management's commitment to maintenance to the entire manufacturing organization
        d. Appoint a highly qualified manager to the position of manufacturing maintenance champion
        e. Mandate that all new machines and systems will have the active involvement of maintenance during planning, design, specification, selection, and implementation
    2. Phase II: Establish maintenance function
        a. Document the present maintenance organization, staffing, facilities, equipment, and procedures
        b. Establish or upgrade existing maintenance database
        c. Evaluate present maintenance function
        d. Define who should perform each level of maintenance for each machine or system
        e. Evaluate present personnel and facilities to perform the maintenance established in Step d
        f. Develop maintenance training and education programs for operators and maintenance personnel; implement these programs
        g. Plan, design, specify, purchase, and implement required maintenance facilities and equipment
        h. Establish upgraded maintenance standard operating procedures for all five levels of maintenance; implement these procedures
    3. Phase III: Manage maintenance functions
        a. Maintain maintenance database
        b. Review machinery and system obsolescence
        c. Participate in new machinery and system planning, design, specification, selection, and implementation
        d. Upgrade training and education of all operators and maintenance personnel
        e. Follow maintenance standard operating procedures
        f. Identify maintenance problems and take corrective action

XV. **Material Flow**. Material flow must be efficient (Chapter 15)
    A. Material flow requirements as the basis for material handling systems

MATERIAL FLOW REQUIREMENTS===>MATERIAL HANDLING SYSTEM
(MATERIAL + FLOW)===>(METHOD)
(WHAT + WHERE + WHEN)===>(HOW + WHO)

B. A major problem in traditional manufacturing is that material handling systems are being designed based upon obsolete specifications of material flow requirements

C. $\underset{\text{MOVES}}{S}$ [WHY (WHAT + WHERE + WHEN)]===>(HOW + WHO)

D. Once material flow is specified for winning manufacturing, then the following obsolete material handling system design guidelines must be eliminated
    1. The best material handling is no material handling
    2. The shorter the distance traveled, the better the flow
    3. Straight-line material flow paths are best
    4. Handle all loads in as large a unit load as possible

E. Continuous flow manufacturing. Frequent movement of small unit loads
    1. Standardize unit loads and material handling equipment
    2. Eliminate, whenever possible, intermediate material handling steps
    3. Minimize the number of material handling steps
    4. Combine the material handling step with the processing step
    5. When manual material handling is most economical, minimize the amount of manual activity by minimizing walking, travel distances, and motions
    6. Eliminate manual handling by mechanizing or automating material handling whenever economically justified
    7. Review all floor space and overhead space for effective utilization
    8. Integrate material flow and information flow whenever feasible
    9. Integrate the flow of materials from distributed receiving to focused factories, through focused departments, to other focused factories, to distributed shipping into one material handling system
    10. Be creative in establishing the most adaptable, maintainable, and responsive material handling system

F. How to establish efficient material flow
    1. Define the objectives and the scope of the material handling system
    2. Establish the material flow requirements; verify that these requirements are consistent with winning manufacturing
    3. Generate alternative material handling system designs for meeting the material flow requirements
    4. Evaluate alternative material handling system designs
    5. Select the preferred material handling system design
    6. Establish an improvement plan
    7. Obtain support for the improvement plan
    8. Implement the preferred material handling system
    9. Audit system's performance and refine as necessary

XVI. **Material Tracking and Control**. Material tracking and control systems must be upgraded (Chapter 16).

A. Responsive, continuous-flow manufacturing cannot function without upgraded material tracking and control systems

B. Material tracking and control systems in winning manufacturing are very different from material tracking and control systems in traditional manufacturing

C. The functions of winning-manufacturing material tracking and control systems are similar to the functions of traditional-manufacturing material tracking and control systems; the major difference is the response time

D. Material tracking and control system (Figure 49)

E. Virtually all unit loads moved will be tracked by automatic identification

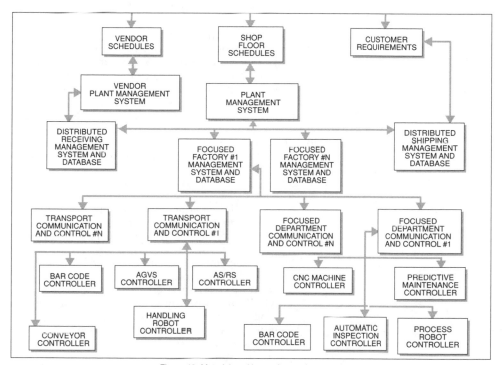

Figure 49. Material tracking and control system

F. Vendors and customers will be integrated just as two focused factories in a plant are integrated; this integration is called electronic data interchange

G. How to upgrade material tracking and control systems

1. The upgrade of the material tracking and control system must be done in conjunction with the creation of winning manufacturing

2. Prior to addressing any specific upgrades to the material tracking and control system, the following must be defined

a. The overall approach to material tracking and control

b. The overall computer system architecture
3. Based upon these top-level designs, the following steps should be pursued
 a. Document the present material tracking and control system
 b. Establish a functional specification
 c. Define alternative approaches
 d. Evaluate alternative approaches
 e. Select the best approach
 f. Develop and implement plan
 g. Obtain support for the project
 h. Implement a pilot project
 i. Audit the project
 j. Implement the total material tracking and control system

XVII. **Human Resources**. Every manager must be dedicated to creating an environment where every employee is motivated and happy (Chapter 17).
 A. For a company to be a winning company, it should
  1. Hire employees who believe they are winners
  2. Create an environment where every employee is motivated and happy so that winners remain winners
 B. The creation of an environment where every employee is motivated and happy requires training, education, and trust
 C. The terms *training* and *education* lead to misunderstanding; therefore, use the term *development*
 D. What development is needed?
  1. Visionary development. Understanding winning manufacturing
  2. General development. Consists of general knowledge and general skills
   a. General knowledge development includes
    i. How your company is organized
    ii. The technology involved with your manufacturing operations
    iii. How your products are used
    iv. Who uses your products
    v. Your company's competition
    vi. Your company's strengths, weaknesses, opportunities, and challenges
   b. General skill development includes
    i. Problem solving
    ii. Planning
    iii. Cost reduction
    iv. Quality enhancement
    v. Communications
    vi. Managing
    vii. Goal setting
    viii. Creativity
    ix. Computer literacy
  3. Specific development
 E. How should development be achieved?
  1. Basic approach
   a. Uncover. Uncover the need for development
   b. Discover. Discover new knowledge or skills
   c. Recover. Put new knowledge or skills into practice

     2. A wide variety of tools should be used to develop all employees

F. Trust

     1. From trust comes respect

     2. From respect comes a sincere desire to listen

     3. Listening results in understanding

     4. Understanding results in concern

     5. Concern results in participation

     6. Participation results in success

     7. Success results in positive reinforcement

     8. Positive reinforcement makes employees happy, and motivates them to work for further positive reinforcement

G. If there is trust, there is no problem with the term *employees*

H. How to create an environment where every employee is motivated and happy

     1. Winning manufacturing is the approach to creating an environment where every employee is motivated and happy

     2. Achieving winning manufacturing requires

          a. A lasting commitment to winning manufacturing

          b. The confidence of all employees in the lasting commitment to winning manufacturing

          c. The development of all employees

          d. A mutual trust among all employees

          e. The cooperation and teamwork of all employees

XVIII. **Team players.** Everyone associated with manufacturing must work together as a team (Chapter 18).

A. Upper management must set the tone for teamwork by mandating and setting an example that clearly indicates

     1. The enemy is the competition, not the vendors, the organization, or the customers

     2. Achieving winning manufacturing requires the teamwork of all vendors, all internal functions, and all customers

     3. All adversarial relationships are unacceptable and must be eliminated

B. The guiding principal in establishing the supplier-customer relationship should be the golden rule: treat your vendors like you desire to be treated by your customers

C. Relationships with suppliers and customers should be based upon

     1. Friendship

     2. Limited sources

     3. Long-term relationships

     4. Quality

     5. Integration

     6. Schedules

     7. Joint improvement process

D. Teamwork within an organization

     1. All organizational units must be 100% directed towards the success of the total organization

     2. There will be no adversarial relationships within the organization

     3. All back-biting politics, one-upmanship, power plays, and so on will be eliminated

     4. All organizational units will function as a cohesive unit

E. How to develop a winning manufacturing team
    1. Identify a leader
    2. Identify team players
        a. Do the players really want to be a part of the team?
        b. Do the players have the abilities that are required by the team?
        c. Are the players truly committed to the success of the team?
    3. Specify the characteristics of a winning manufacturing team
        a. Shared vision
        b. Shared values
        c. Shared expectations
        d. Shared commitment
        e. Shared confidence
        f. Shared responsibility
        g. Shared rewards
    4. Establish cooperation
    5. Establish a plan
    6. Obtain success
    7. Build upon success; return to Step 4.

XIX. **Simplification**. All manufacturing must be simplified (Chapter 19).
    A. Manufacturing must be streamlined
    B. Manufacturing must be better understood
    C. Simplified product design
        1. The reduction of the number of parts in a product
        2. Use of standard parts
    D. Simplified manufacturing processes and operating systems will result from pursuing winning manufacturing; in brief, traditional manufacturing is complex, winning manufacturing is simple
    E. Simplified organizational structures are needed in winning manufacturing
    F. A typical winning manufacturing organization chart will consist of four layers
    G. How to simplify manufacturing
        1. Winning manufacturing is simplified manufacturing; simplified product design, manufacturing processes, and operating system will result from pursuing winning manufacturing
        2. Simplified organizational structure will result from taking the following steps
            a. As the process of winning manufacturing begins, the ultimate structure should be established
            b. Compare the ultimate organizational structure with the existing organizational structure; where more layers exist than should ultimately exist, implement a hiring freeze
            c. As people leave the company, realignment should occur in the direction of the ultimate structure
            d. Establish a schedule for implementing the ultimate organizational structure

XX. **Integration**. All organization and operations must be integrated (Chapter 20).
    A. Integration is the combining of elements to form a whole
    B. Due to synergy that results from combining elements, the

benefits achieved from integration far exceed the benefits which result from the summation of the elements.

C. Prerequisites of winning manufacturing integration

    1. Dynamic consistency

        a. Elements can only be integrated if they have a consistent mission

        b. Integration can only survive when the elements that are being combined are allowed to be dynamic

    2. Interface standards

        a. Material handling interface standards must be established to include unit load size, weight, and identification

        b. Communication interface standards must define the information protocol

D. Figure 50. Integration's role in winning manufacturing

E. Integrated organizations

    1. Integrated internal systems–Computer Integrated Manufacturing (CIM)

        a. The essence of CIM is that by using standard information protocols and an integrated corporate database, communications within an organization will be improved

        b. A responsive, adaptable, and reliable computer system must support CIM

        c. All CIM information must be quality information

        d. CIM implementation will be straightforward

        e. CIM must encompass an entire manufacturing company

        f. CIM must be designed top-down

        g. CIM will be the integration of the functions of manufacturing through the use of the computer, not the integration of computers

        h. CIM is a long-term strategy

        i. CIM must be based on a methodical plan

    2. Integrated employees. Trusted employees who work as a team are required to achieve winning manufacturing (Chapters 17 and 18)

    3. Integrated external systems. Vendors and customers must be integrated via electronic data interchange (Chapter 16).

    4. Integrated vendors and customers. The application of the golden rule will create teamwork (Chapter 18)

    5. Integrated global philosophy. The global marketplace must be treated as an integrated portion of its domestic business (Chapter 5)

F. Integrated operations

    1. Integrated product development (Chapter 4)

    2. Integrated factory (Chapter 9)

    3. Integrated manufacturing management (Chapter 21)

G. How to integrate organizations and operations

    1. Confirm that the twenty Requirements of Success are your company's vision of where your organization is heading

    2. Define interface standards that include operational, procedural, computer, organizational, and measurement standards

    3. Pursue specific Requirements of Success while considering all twenty requirements and the interface standards

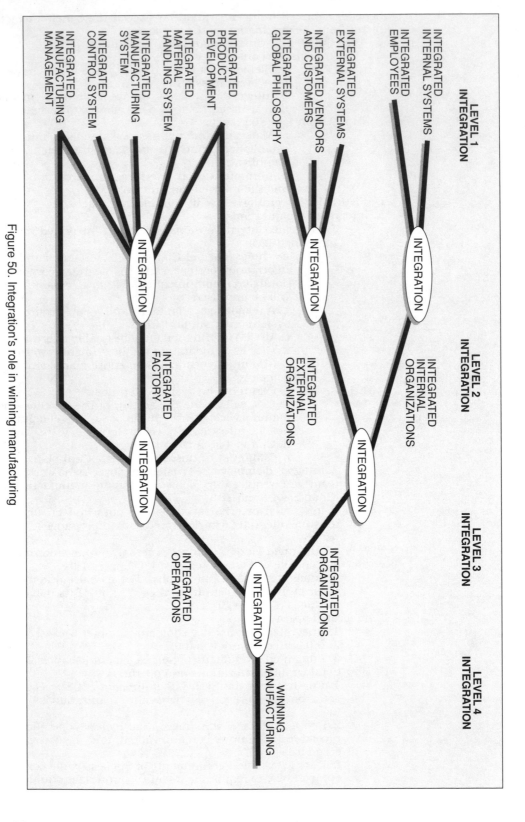

Figure 50. Integration's role in winning manufacturing

220

4. Implement improvements for the specific Requirements of Success

5. Integrated improved operations with ongoing improved operations

6. Repeat Steps 3, 4, and 5; continue to pursue improvements and winning manufacturing

XXI. **Understanding**. Manufacturing management must understand winning manufacturing (Chapter 21).

A. Fundamentals of winning manufacturing

1. A prerequisite of winning manufacturing is a commitment to winning

2. A prerequisite of winning manufacturing is technical intimacy

B. Manufacturing management must reject

1. Fads, gimmicks, and quick fixes

2. Fire-fighting and short-term optimization

3. Incremental analysis

4. Petty politics and adversarial relationships

C. All levels of management must have strong technical, human, and conceptual skills

D. All twenty Requirements of Success must be understood to achieve winning manufacturing

E. Winning manufacturing requires leadership; the winning manufacturing team leader will

1. Be certain everyone has a shared vision of winning manufacturing

2. Make sure everyone has a clear understanding of their responsibilities

3. Create an environment where people want to participate

4. Make certain that the right people are doing the right jobs

5. Be visible in support and setting an example, but invisible in decision making, except where needed, and in obtaining recognition

6. Assure that the right people receive proper recognition

7. Understand that each person has a different motivation, perspective, and objective, and that each must be guided and encouraged differently

8. Have wide-angle vision and understand the big picture of where an operation is headed

9. Have the ability to look beyond the problems of the present operations and focus on the opportunities of the future

10. Through enthusiasm, create excitement and urgency among the team members

11. Be an excellent listener

12. Do not procrastinate

13. Be driven by a desire for continuous improvement

14. Be interested in obtaining an adequate return on investment, but also be interested in doing what will ensure the firm's success

15. Be certain that all decisions are made by the appropriate level in the organization

F. All employees of a manufacturing company pursuing winning manufacturing should be team members whose responsibilities are to

1. Adopt the shared vision of winning manufacturing
2. Understand how their tasks are affected by the shared vision of winning manufacturing
3. Continuously improve their tasks within the context of the shared vision of winning manufacturing
4. Work with other team members to improve the integration of tasks
5. Participate with other team members and leaders for the improvement of the company
6. Communicate with leaders on opportunities for improvement
7. Be accountable for the implementation of improvements
8. Accept full ownership of improvements
9. Accept full responsibility for decisions best made by them
10. Be an enthusiastic team player

G. How to facilitate manufacturing management understanding of winning manufacturing

1. Phase I: Winning Manufacturing Awareness
   a. Identify a winning manufacturing pioneer
   b. Study this book
   c. Do a preliminary prioritization of the Requirements of Success
   d. Send an introductory memo to management
   e. Conduct a one-hour winning manufacturing review meeting
2. Phase II: Winning Manufacturing Commitment; Conduct a winning manufacturing commitment meeting so management understands winning manufacturing

XXII.   **A Call to Action**

A. Phase I: Winning Manufacturing Awareness
   1. Action Ia: Identify the winning manufacturing pioneer
   2. Action Ib: The pioneer should study this book and fully understand winning manufacturing
   3. Action Ic: Conduct a winning manufacturing review meeting (see Appendix A)
   4. Action Id: Manufacturing management should read *Winning Manufacturing*

B. Phase II: Winning Manufacturing Commitment
   1. Action IIa: Conduct a winning manufacturing commitment meeting (see Appendix B)
   2. Action IIb: Obtain manufacturing management's commitment to winning manufacturing
   3. Action IIc: Appoint a winning manufacturing chairman.
   4. Action IId: Establish a date for the initiation of the winning manufacturing visionary development process

C. Phase III: Winning Manufacturing Visionary Development
   1. Action IIIa: Assign all employees to a visionary development group
   2. Action IIIb: Conduct a winning manufacturing orientation briefing
   3. Action IIIc: Conduct a winning manufacturing management seminar
   4. Action IIId: Initiate winning manufacturing study groups

D. Phase IV: Winning Manufacturing Planning
   1. Action IVa: Distribute, collect, and summarize the manufacturing management priorities questionnaire. (Figure 1)

       2. Action IVb: Conduct a winning manufacturing prioritization meeting (Appendix C)

       3. Action IVc: Conduct a winning manufacturing Requirement of Success initiation meeting for each prioritized Requirement of Success (see Appendix D)

       4. Action IVd: Establish a team for each prioritized Requirement of Success

   E. Phase V: Winning Manufacturing Execution

       1. Action Va: Assess present status and identify specific goals

       2. Action Vb: Identify and evaluate alternative approaches

       3. Action Vc: Define and obtain support for improvement plans

       4. Action Vd: Implement plans and audit results

   F. Go make something happen!

APPROACH 4
WINNING MANUFACTURING STUDY GROUPS

I. OBJECTIVE:	The same as the objective of the winning manufacturing seminar. The only differences are: 1. The study groups will meet for one to two hours per week over many months. 2. The study groups will be much more participative than the winning manufacturing management seminar.
II. STUDY GROUP LEADERS:	A shop floor leader who has attended the winning manufacturing management seminar
III. MEETING PREPARATION:	All participants should have attended the winning manufacturing orientation briefing and should be reading *Winning Manufacturing.*
IV. PARTICIPANTS:	Shop floor personnel (Group IV)
V. DURATION:	One to two hours per week for as many weeks as it takes to cover all of *Winning Manufacturing*
VI. WEEKLY AGENDA:	A. Winning Manufacturing B. Method of pursuing winning manufacturing C. Status report D. Presentation of one or two Requirements of Success E. Opportunities for pursuing specific Requirements of Success F. Open discussion G. Assignment of action items
VII. STUDY GROUP HANDOUTS:	The handout for each week should be the relevant portion of the winning manufacturing management seminar handout.